Beyond the Revelation

The Last Eden

Unless otherwise specified, all Scriptures are taken from the King James Version of the Holy Bible.

BEYOND THE REVELATION
© 2009 by Terry Gayle Alexander

All rights reserved under International Copyright Law. No part of this book may be used or reproduced in any manner whatsoever without written permission of the publisher, except in the case of brief quotations in articles and reviews. For more information write: Bible Belt Publishing, 500 Beacon Dr., Oklahoma City, OK 73127, (800) 652-1144, *www.biblebeltpublishing.com.*

Printed in the United States of America

ISBN 1-933641-36-3

Beyond the Revelation

The Last Eden

Elder Gayle Alexander

Dedication

To Jesus Christ, for without the light of His Word, we would have no knowledge of the things that should have been written.

To my wife Nell, who has been my faithful wife for forty-seven-plus years, since age sixteen. Her advice and work in grammatics and proofreading on this manuscript have proved to be of untold value to this work.

To many other brothers and sisters in Christ who have encouraged me with kind words in this effort. I praise the Most High God for each and every one!

To Southwest Radio Ministries for their corageous fight to warn the masses with the true message of God in these last days. There is no value you can put on being a Watchman on the Wall when the enemy is raging at the gate. Their prophetic outreach is unmatched in this land.

—Elder Terry Gayle Alexander

Contents

Preface 9

Foreword 11

Introduction 13

The First Adam Loses the First Eden 25

The Journey Begins 37

Look Dad, There's Giants Out There 52

From Ararat to Goshen 68

From Goshen to the Kingdom 92

Will The King Be Revealed? 122

Jesus Christ Is Israel's God, After All! 144

New Beginnings 166

Epilogue: Eight Sevens of Revelation 179

Addendum A: Temples in Scripture 185

Addendum B: Born Again? 192

In Closing 195

Preface

I feel the only way we can understand what our wonderful God did to preserve the human family (after the fall into sin) is to go back to the beginning and follow Adam's *moving* story to the end. In so doing, we will find many tentacles, with each leading to the same consummation: The Last Eden. Because this is a story about moving, I hope to follow some of these tentacles in this manuscript. This great story has been bearing on my mind for some time. I am very glad God has (in these last few months) permitted me to finish in His time and for His glory. The story of Adam and his quest to be returned to this Last Eden is a beautiful story that could only be orchestrated and told by our Holy God, who in the prophetic Word recorded the end of all history. In order to know the end of all history, we must read the words of the One who wrote it down as He saw it happening.

I take no credit for one single sentence of this story, because, in reality, God Himself wrote it by His amazing grace. As I have stated, this manuscript is just a story about *moving*: Adam *moving* from The First Eden to The Last Eden. However, let us all be reminded: This story is actually about us.

I will take credit for the references to my personal life when as a backward hillbilly boy (who "like Adam" was always *moving*), I grew to my mid-teens. I can only hope you will find these to be enjoyable as I attempt to relate a few things in my early life to some of the early scenes in the Book of Genesis. I am convinced that Tubal-cain and my Dad had at least a few things in common when it came to making implements for tilling the soil.

I am totally convinced if he could have, Satan would have destroyed the good genes (seed) of Adam, Noah, Abraham, David, etc., preventing the birth of the promised Messiah, Jesus Christ through the virgin Mary, who was the promised lineage of David (according to the flesh)! We know from the Scripture, Satan will not give up until he is defeated at Armageddon and bound. He will be permanently cast into the lake of fire a thousand years later!

Also, I hope you will enjoy Chapter Five (one of the tentacles of this seven thousand-year *moving story*) which is quite revealing on just how and why God is permitting "wealth" to accumulate in this world. Also, how this "wealth" has in the past and will in the future be used for God's purpose and pleasure.

I hope you will enjoy the "Eight Sevens" of Revelation in the Epilogue and "Temples in Scripture" in the addendum at the close of the manuscript.

Now, let's join (our father) Adam on his *long journey* from the First Eden, **Beyond the Revelation,** into, **The Last Eden.**

—Elder Terry Gayle Alexander

Foreword

Recently I was utterly amazed to read from a 75-page research paper by Major Brian Stuckert, published under the authority and commendation of the School of Advanced Military Studies, United States Army Command and General Staff College, under the title *Strategic Implications of American Millennialism.*

Evidently there are many in the higher echelons of our government, and foreign governments as well, who believe, or at least try to believe, that we premillennial Christians are the motivators and participators in a conspiracy to join with Israel to force all nations into a last world war, or Armageddon, in order to bring back Israel's Messiah and our own Lord Jesus Christ. We certainly compliment the major in his research in seemingly connecting all the dots.

However, are we actually motivators and participants in such a panoramic, mystic scheme? Or, are we simply spectators in a world arena watching the actors on a stage read and act out their parts in a prophetic drama written over a period of 1,600 years by prophets like Joel, Jeremiah, Ezekiel, Amos, Zechariah, Jesus, and the Apostle John?

There is a rocky, bumpy, muddy, winding, and at times, uncertain road that winds through 66 books of the Bible, over a period of 6,000 years travel time, from the First Eden to the Last Eden. We are now nearing the last and most dangerous sections of this road.

What my good friend, Brother Terry Alexander, has done in this book is to travel this road with us until we reach that blessed and holy city where there will be no hunger, no tears, no sorrow, no sin, no crime, no sickness, no disappointments, not even a red light. We can read in the Holy Scriptures the promised blessings of God awaiting us in the New Jerusalem, the Paradise of God. But the Bible indicates that this is only a partial list, and that you and I cannot even begin to imagine what lies beyond the last verse in Revelation.

"But as it is written, Eye hath not seen, nor ear heard, neither have **entered into the heart of man,** the things which God hath prepared for them that love him" (1 Corinthians 2:9).

This book will take you through time, space, and places in God's eternal kingdom that you may never have traveled before. Take my word for it.

Introduction

As we look at Isaiah 51:3, we notice a very revealing statement our Holy God emphasizes concerning His future plans for this planet.

> For the LORD shall comfort Zion: He will comfort **all** her waste places; and He **will** make **her wilderness like Eden, and her desert like the garden of the LORD;** joy and gladness **shall** be found therein, thanksgiving, and the voice of melody.

Ezekiel 36:33–36 continues:

> Thus saith the Lord God; In the day that I shall have cleansed you [Israel] from all your iniquities, **I will** also cause you to dwell in the cities, and the **wastes shall be builded.** And the **desolate land shall be tilled,** whereas it lay desolate in the sight of all that passed by. And they shall say, This land that was desolate is become **like the garden of Eden;** and the waste and desolate and ruined cities are become fenced, and are inhabited. Then the heathen that are left [after Armageddon] round about you shall know that **I the LORD** build the ruined places, and plant that that was desolate: **I the LORD have spoken it and I will do it.**

Also, Romans 8:21–23 informs us of this transformation:

> Because the **creature** [creature/creation same in the Greek: Ktis'is[1]] itself also **shall** be delivered from the bondage of corruption into the glorious liberty of the children of God. For we know that the whole **creation** groaneth and travaileth in pain together until now. And not only they, but ourselves also, which have the first fruits of the Spirit, even we ourselves groan within ourselves waiting for the adoption to wit, **the redemption of our body** (emphasis and commentary mine).

What an exciting time to be alive in the twenty-first century A.D. with prophecy being fulfilled on every part of the globe! Israel is back in **her land** promised by God over 2,750 years ago and, no doubt, these three prophecies I have just mentioned in the Scriptural Books of Ezekiel, Isaiah, and Romans are looming on the horizon.

Surely, the angel that will blow the trumpet announcing the rapture is taking daily practice for this one-time event. We know the trump will sound and the dead in Christ shall be raised incorruptible and the living in Christ shall be changed. At that time, God will give His saved people a body that pleases Him. Thank you, Lord!

First John 3:2 breaks the waiting silence of our thoughts with this admonition. We read: "Beloved, **now** are we the sons of God, and it doth not yet appear what we shall be: but we know that, when He shall appear, **we shall be like Him;** for we shall see Him as He is" (emphasis mine).

Jesus walked through walls and flew to the third Heaven to His Father "after His resurrection." Knowing God's Words are true, after the resurrection, the true Church Saints (when we are like Him) will be able to do the same.

---

1. James Strong, *Strong's Exhaustive Concordance*.

It has been over two thousand years since God the Holy Ghost overshadowed the womb of a tender virgin named Mary and caused the miraculous conception and birth of the Savior of all mankind. Who would have dreamed the great God of this universe would have spared this evil world and granted us the wonderful privilege of life and living to this present time in human history? We have a longsuffering and patient God who, beyond all human comprehension, loves His creation. However, I fear, as it has in the past, His longsuffering and patience is wearing thin in these last days of apostasy and perversion. America and the nations of the world cannot continue on this downward track without (sometime in the future) receiving the judgment and wrath of a Holy God. With prophecy fulfillment at an all-time high, I truly feel the day of His appearing to rapture His Church could soon become reality. It seems to me the possibility exists that as we move further into the present worldwide economic situation, this dilemma just may be the catalyst to propel Satan's man to his predicted position in the near future.

If this is true, we on Planet Earth could be presently moving very close to what the prophets call (depending on where you read in God's Words):

» The Day of the Lord (Isaiah 2:12)
» The Day of God (2 Pet. 3:12)
» The Day of the Lord Jesus Christ (1 Cor. 1:8)
» The Day of Christ (2 Thessalonians 2:2)
» That Great Day of God Almighty (Rev. 16:14)

I have noticed in the last forty years of my reading Bible literature and study of Scripture that many authors and Bible commentators try to separate these events to augment their particular Scriptural scenario (especially on the subject of the rapture). In doing so, it seems (at least in my thinking) they possibly separate the very principle of what God is saying. I do not say this to be critical, but to make a point of Scripture. Jesus Christ told Philip in John 14:9b, "he that hath seen me hath seen the Father; and how sayest thou then, Shew us the Father?"

Realizing that Jesus is God, I think possibly a better rendering of these references would be that they are all speaking of one day: God's Day of judgment and peace. We can read in 2 Peter 3:10,12 exactly when this Day of God ends:

> But the **day of the Lord** will come as a thief in the night; **in the which** [denotes within, into, or among[2]] the heavens shall pass away with a great noise, and the elements shall melt with fervent heat, **the earth also and the works that are therein shall be burned up** [No earth, no day of the Lord on the earth].... Looking for and hasting unto the coming of the **day of God, wherein** [in which time[3]] **the heavens being on fire shall be dissolved** (let loose[4]) **and the elements shall melt with fervent heat.**

With the word "wherein" and the phrase "in the which," what is the Apostle Peter saying about this one event, since he used both terms, "day of God" and "day of the LORD"?

We know from reading Revelation 20:9,11 the earth doesn't dissolve with fervent heat until the end of the thousand-year millennium.[5]

Also, 2 Peter 3:8 tells us that one day is with the Lord as a thousand years, and a thousand years as one day. So, I guess the $64,000 question is: When does God's "Day" begin?

---
2. Noah Webster, *American Dictionary of the English Language*
3. Ibid.
4. Ibid.
5. Reference page one, Chapter 8 "Quote" by Dr. Henry Morris in this manuscript.

Does Jesus Christ begin His Day at the rapture of the church to Heaven (1 Thessalonians 4:13-18), or at His Revelation "to the earth" from Heaven (Rev. 19:11-21)? You decide.

But, beware: Five times in the little Book of Joel, God's Word uses the term "day of the Lord," and not one Verse is speaking of the millennium, the very place the Apostle Peter lets us know the Day of the Lord will end. Do you think we should back up a little farther and take a look at the rapture of the church as a possible beginning point for the Day of the Lord? Maybe so; give it some thought.

Whether you believe in a pre-tribulation rapture, mid-tribulation rapture, pre-wrath rapture, post-tribulation rapture, or some kind of rapture I, nor anyone else, has ever heard of, it would seem to me that the Lord Jesus Christ's Day would begin when He takes over at the end of the Dispensation of Grace.

We should note the title deed of Planet Earth is handed to the Lord Jesus Christ very early in Chapter Five of the Book of Revelation.

Later in this manuscript we will be looking at this great Day of our God and Savior Jesus Christ with much more detail as we travel through the Holy Scriptures on our way **back to the Last Eden.**

It does seem the Dispensation of God's amazing Grace is swiftly coming to a close, and the nations of Planet Earth are doing all they can to speed up the process of entering into this "day," no matter what Scripture you use or how you apply them. As we watch and observe from the seat of our Biblical understanding, the existing systems of this world come closer and closer each day to becoming one system. It is very obvious. Something is in the making prophetically!

The United Nations is promoting a **one-world government.** Megachurch leaders in America and around the world (which make the claim they are going to bring back the Christ) are promoting a **one-world church.** The many treaties the nations of the world have signed and are putting into practice suggest a **one-world economy** is already on the horizon!

Note: I could not help noticing on our last tour to Petra in southern Jordan that our tour guide made the comment that a United Nations organization was installing water and electricity into this valley of the mountains. This brought Zechariah 14:5 and Daniel 11:41 to mind concerning the remnant of Israel and their fleeing in the middle of the tribulation period.

I am compelled to believe the question should be asked: Just what kind of christ are these world religions and the United Nations planning to bring back? With all these other entities already in place, he may just be Antichrist!

When I look at the many prophecies in God's Holy Word having been fulfilled in my lifetime, I am forced to conclude that world leaders are out of control and Satan is doing all he can to bring the **religious,** the **economic,** and **governmental** systems together in order to be ready for this future incarnate Antichrist. **Seemingly, these things have gone into overdrive since I started working on this manuscript.** Surely, no one believes that the financial status of this many world economies failed at once without the international bankers having their hands in the process.

Years ago, as I grew up in a rural farm setting in the hills of Middle Tennessee, I would never have dreamed these things would so quickly have come to pass. In those days (late 1940s) one of the greatest challenges a young Tennessee hillbilly boy and his two sisters might have faced could have been milking a Jersey cow on a cold winter's morning. The metal bail of the milk pail would stick to your hand and pull off the skin after milking the warm and wet udder of Old Browney (the Jersey cow). I also remember this task of milking Old Browney would be made even more difficult if she had been wading through the cockleburr patch (called "cuckleburr" in the hillbilly tongue) before milking time. Her tail would almost become a lethal weapon during the fall and winter months, which would knock you off the milk stool, especially if the cockleburrs were frozen in a mixture of cow dung and hair!

Also as a young farm boy, I remember swinging from one bank of a large ravine (gulley in the hillbilly tongue) to the other bank (which I often did on a grapevine cut loose from its roots). This feat had worked well in times past, but on this particular day I attempted to hold my "brand-new" Red Rider Carbine BB gun in one hand and hold the grapevine with the other arm and hand! I have often thought as I have grown older that I must have seen one too many Tarzan movies on my Uncle John's new black-and-white twenth-one inch television set. Nevertheless, I made the attempt and, with bark flying, I slid down the grapevine and fell about fifteen feet to the bottom of this large gulley. When I finally landed on my backside my breath was totally gone, but my life was spared by the love and grace of God. As I turned my head and body back and forth to try to get my breath, I saw a long, sharp-tipped Black Locust limb someone had cut off with a chopping axe just a few inches to my right. This limb was very well attached to a large, dead Black Locust tree trunk that was lying in the bottom of this gulley. The limb was protruding upward at the same angle that the trunk of my body had fallen. Had I have fallen fifteen or twenty inches to the right, this limb would have penetrated the whole trunk of my body (from the bottom upward). Surely you get the point?

As an unsaved, accountable-to-God individual, I still remember wondering (at that time) where I would have been for eternity if I had fallen a few inches to the right.

Also, my sisters and I might have faced another dilemma

of falling off Old Browney as we attempted to ride her bareback off the steep hills which were on Aunt Callie's farm. Our thinking might have been: "Well, we have seen the people on Uncle John's new television do it 'out West,' so, why couldn't we do it here 'in the East'?"

In those days of adventure back on my Aunt Callie's hillside farm, the gullies were deep and those hills were steep. It is somewhat miraculous that we were not killed or at least wounded for life. I personally feel that God's loving angels must have worked overtime as they overshadowed both my sisters and I.

Back in those days, my parents were too poor to own much property of their own, but none of us kids knew we were poor. We never asked why my father rented from my Aunt Callie. In those days, the terms self-esteem, the power of self, live-your-dream, diversity, etc. were not known or taught on Lox Creek where we lived. In 1955 my father (after landing a job at an aerospace factory in 1951) purchased his first decent car, and in 1957 his first really livable home. This home was near the small Middle Tennessee town in which I now reside. Dad was forty-two years old at this time. How things have changed!

But today is a new era and the trivial things of yesterday seem like a Sunday afternoon picnic when compared to what is facing the world and its' inhabitants today. Today, people are facing things like $300,000-$3,000,000 home loan foreclosures, AIDS, national genocide, pollution of every description, and being poisoned by the very food we consume.

Abortion is a national sin, and evolution is deceiving millions from the truth of God's Word into eternal ruin! Amen.

Terrorism is rampant and all nations are affected by the scourge of those who murder in the name of their god or other organizations. World War III seems eminent.

While politicians spend most of their time getting re-elected, illegal aliens have consumed a large number of America's social programs, and are threatening to bankrupt the nation as a whole.

As already noted, since I began this manuscript America and most of the world has suffered possibly the greatest financial debacle of all time. I personally believe this debacle was created by those who want to further their desires for a one world order. Time will tell if I am correct.

We don't know anymore what we are eating and drinking because almost all our food source comes from a can or bottle. A large portion of these cans and bottles come from some foreign country. However, we are also experiencing death and mayhem from our own food processors as they cripple and kill our population with such things as tainted peanut products.

Our childrens' toys are not only laden with lead on the outside; but, are laden with seductive, mythical, satanic natures within their being. And, television commercials should definitely be rated "XXX."

"Made in China" has quickly become a household phrase when only a few short years ago a large number of Chinese were still living in shanties and riding bicycles for transportation. Also, China now has over four hundred skyscrapers, many of which are taller than any in the United States! What happened? Is China the country John saw in Revelation 9:13–21 that will slay the third part of men on planet Earth? Also, **why** does China now own a large part of America's debt? I remember reading that a world famous financier once said, "Give me control of a country's finance and I care not what laws they may pass!" When I was growing up on Lox Creek, I often heard my parents make the statement, "Well, we know who controls the purse strings in that house." Does anyone other than me wonder if China is preparing for a 200,000,000 man march toward the Middle East?

Oil has been pushed over the $100-a-barrel mark and then declined. Gasoline has been over $4 per gallon and has also declined. However, oil tycoons are getting richer and bragging about it, while we on the lower end of the totem pole who use their products are getting poorer!

I remember in the mid-1960s, you could purchase gasoline for less than 25 cents per gallon in Middle Tennessee. Those days are only a memory now.

Not long ago when Wally World first came on the scene, its' founder prided himself with the phrase *"Made in America."* Now, this same Wally World has located throughout the world and forgotten its founding principals. How sad!

As we in America strain more each year to "beat out" our existence on Planet Earth, it seems that the God who created Planet Earth attempts more and more each year to make a statement to us with Earth's floods, droughts, hurricanes, tornadoes, wildfires, ice storms, and other natural disasters. It would not surprise me if our wonderful God is using nature and other elements to try to tell His favorite creation, the human family: "Hey, look up for your redemption is in Heaven and I will soon tell Him to come down to the air and call His Church up to meet Him." Remember 1 Thessalonians 4:13.

As we *move* farther and farther into this twenty-first century on our *journey* to go **Beyond the Revelation and reach The Last Eden,** it seems that man is attempting to believe the unbelievable, fix the unfixable, reach for the unobtainable, dream about that which is mythical, and attempt that which only God Himself can accomplish. In short, mankind (through Lucifer) is trying to rebuild Babel as a world kingdom, do a much better job than Nimrod, and invade God's domain (outer space) in the process.

I remember in the late 1940s, as I was only four to five years old, I would repeatedly dream the same dream. As I lay asleep in my bed, I would dream I was flying over the valley to the south of the small two-room home where my Dad, Mom, two sisters, and, of course, myself, lived across from my Pappy and Mammy. This dream would reoccur night after night, with usually about the same flight pattern but guess what? The first time this author flew a real flight pattern was some twenty-two years later in 1967 when the company I worked for sent me to Long Island, New York, on a work assignment. I flew inside a Boeing 707 (not on the outside)! There was no fantasy involved. The flight was real and I was really scared!

The sad fact in today's world is: The majority of peoples thrive on fantasy and pretense. (Global warming is a good example.)

The Words of our God tells us plainly in Jeremiah 23:28a: "The prophet that hath a dream, let him tell a dream; and he that hath my word, let him speak my word faithfully. . . ." We must never confuse human dreams and fantasy visions with the pure words of a holy God.

What will be the end of this dilemma in our present world which man has created by listening to the devil? God's prophets have not been silent, especially for the past thirty-five hundred years on this matter and we (in the closing scenes of this Dispensation of God's wonderful Grace) would do well to read and study these prophets carefully. **Only the Holy Bible** has dependable prophecy recorded over this period. Throughout human history God's Holy Bible has proven itself to be true one hundred percent of the time. No other religious writings on the planet can come close to this track record; therefore, we would do well to regularly examine the Holy Bible's 774,747 Words, its 31,173 Verses, its 1,189 Chapters, its 66 Books.[6]

I would at this time like to begin a *journey* from the First

---

6. Wilmington, H. L. *Wilmington's Complete Guide to Bible Knowledge*

Garden of Eden in the Book of Genesis, and go through the Holy Bible examining many of the wonderful things God's holy prophets have to say on this most important subject of going ***Beyond the Revelation* into *The Last Eden.***

Also, we will look at the many attempts by the devil to destroy this promised Seed (Jesus Christ) in order that he might stop God's salvation from being given to mankind at Calvary! Without this salvation being in place, no one would be able to enter "the Second Eden" and live forever.

Also, I think you may be very surprised at some of the subtle attempts Lucifer made in the first four thousand years in his quest to eventually be God, and I assure you he is not through.

We must take notice of this one fact. There are many prophecies in the Bible (Gen. 3:15, in particular) that have affected humanity in the past, are affecting us in the present, and will affect *all* the human family in the near future. Therefore, **take note**, because you are included, whether you want to be or not! It matters not if you are as saved as Jesus, or as lost as a ball in high weeds, **prophecy directly affects you!**

In Chapter Five we will examine some of the things our God has done to gather the wealth of this world to accomplish His glorious purpose for Himself and His people: past, present, and future.

As this world moves on the fast track to judgment, and this manuscript takes shape to completion, it is my sincere desire that you will allow me to insert a few more of my life's experiences, as I have in this introduction.

Come along while we take a walk through God's Holy Words and arrive in a world Our Holy God says has become "like" the Garden of Eden. It all lies just *Beyond the Revelation*. Read again Isaiah 51:3, Ezekiel 36:35, and Romans 8:21–23.

—Elder Terry Gayle Alexander

Chapter One

The First Adam Loses the First Eden

As we begin our journey in Chapter One to eventually go *Beyond the Revelation,* we will begin with a question. What is the Revelation of Jesus Christ (Scripturally) and where in the Holy Scriptures would we find this much published event which is taking place?

The answer is quite simple. We know that John, the beloved apostle of Jesus Christ, was given this Revelation in approximately A.D. 96 by an angel whom Jesus Christ had sent from Heaven where Jesus had received it from God the Father.

So the Scriptural sequence of the Book of Revelation is:

» What God the Father gave to Jesus **in Heaven;**
» What Jesus the Son then sent by the angel to John, who received this vision on the Isle of Patmos **on Earth;**
» What John the Apostle then bare record of by writing the inspired Revelation of Jesus Christ **in a Book;**
» What God supernaturally did by placing and preserving that Book last in the canon of scriptures for us to read in the twenty-first century.

Glory! Hallelujah! This should cause even the most placid Christian to at least grunt a "Thank You, Lord." Also, it is noteworthy to add: This whole Book of Revelation is leading up to the literal revealing of Jesus Christ to Planet Earth in Revelation 19:11–21. These are the final Scriptures we will use in Chapter Seven taking us on our journey, *Beyond the Revelation.*

Now, when this Revelation began in the mind of God is a totally different story. We must understand that just because John received this revelation from Jesus Christ in A.D. 96[7] it in no way suggests Jesus Christ began at this time. In fact, the same human author receiving the Revelation from Jesus Christ by His angel wrote by inspiration in A.D. 30[8] these Words. We read John 1:1–5:

> **In the beginning** was **the Word,** and the **Word was with God,** and **the Word was God.** The same was in the beginning with God. All things were made **by him;** and without him was not any thing made that was made. In him was life; and the life was the light of men. And the light shineth in darkness; and the darkness comprehended it not [Emphasis mine].

So, in these Verses we can plainly see that Jesus Christ was in the beginning working in the Godhead as the Word (God said) to complete creation over four thousand years before John was given this revelation on the Isle of Patmos.

To get back to the beginning and start our *journey*, we must go to Genesis 1:1. Here we begin to read of the Triune God in His creative works as He brings into existence in five twenty-four-hour days of creation—from nothing—all of the things it will take to sustain His most precious creation—man—on day six: "Evening, morning, first day; evening, morning, second day, etc."

---

7. Ussher, James. *The Annals of the World*
8. Ibid.

Hebrews 11:3 gives us insight as to how Jesus created all things in six days, from nothing. We read:

> Through faith we understand that the worlds were **framed by the word of God,** so that things which are seen were not made of things which do appear. [See also Exodus 20:11; 31:17] [emphasis mine].

If we take a closer look at this Greek word from which we get our English word framed, *kat-ar-tid'-zo,*[9] we find this definition: "To make perfect; to join together; to prepare; to complete, thoroughly." Reviewing John 1:3 we notice, **all things were made by Him, and without Him was not anything made that was made.**

Someone might ask: "What did Jesus Christ use to make all things?" I believe we can safely say; "things which do not appear!" (Heb.11:3). I remember at a Southwest Radio Ministries Prophecy Conference in the 1990s hearing a very dear friend say that he believed God used "particles of power" to build this universe. I like that definition!

We read of the creative acts of God on day six in Genesis 1:24–27, 31; 2:7:

> And **God said,** Let the earth bring forth the living creature after his kind, cattle, and creeping thing, and beast of the earth after his kind: and it was so. And **God made** the beast of the earth after his kind, and cattle after their kind, and every thing that creepeth upon the earth after his kind: and God saw that it was good. And **God said,** Let us make man in our image, after our likeness: and let them have dominion over the fish of the sea, and over the fowl of the air, and over

---

9. Ibid.

the cattle, and over all the earth, and over every creeping thing that creepeth upon the earth. So **God created** man in his own image, in the image of God created he him; male and female created he them. . . . And **God saw** every thing that he had made, and, behold, it was **very good.** And the evening and the morning were the sixth day. . . . And the LORD **God formed** man of the dust of the ground, and breathed into his nostrils the breath of life; and **man became a living soul** [emphasis mine].

Knowing the nature of our loving God and His desire to fellowship with man, it did not take Him very long (after resting on the seventh day) to begin to walk in His newly created Garden of Eden with His prized creation (Adam). And Even though, Adam had been given the task of naming all the animal-kind and fowl-kind God had created on day six, it seemed to God that Adam was very lonely. It was then God did for Adam what no one else could have done. He caused a deep sleep to come upon Adam and took from his side a rib, and then closed up the flesh thereof. Then, from this rib which God had surgically removed from Adam, He made a help meet (Gen. 2:8) and brought *her* unto the man. Adam named this new creature "woman."

It seemed everything was looking great to this first man (especially his wife, Eve) whom God had placed in this garden paradise on the east of Eden. However, as we all know, it was not to last.

You see, when God placed these first two humans in this First Eden paradise, He gave them **one prohibition,** this being:

And out of the ground made the LORD God to grow every tree that is pleasant to the sight, and good for food; the

tree of life also in the midst of the garden, and the **tree of knowledge of good and evil.** . . . And the LORD God commanded the man, saying, Of **every tree** of the garden **thou mayest freely eat: But of the tree of the knowledge of good and evil, thou shalt not eat of it: for in the day that thou eatest thereof thou shalt surely die.**

—Genesis 2:9, 16–17 [emphasis mine]

It seems that at this point in Scripture a lot of Christians miss a very important fact. God had given Adam, Eve, and their descendants, dominion over all of the creation (Genesis 1:26-28).

As we look at the definition of the word "dominion" in our old *Webster's American Dictionary of the English Language*, we find this meaning revealed: **"Sovereign or supreme authority; The power of governing and controlling; The right of possession and use** *without being accountable.*"

Wow! It is evident Adam had a tremendous amount of responsibility and power placed on his shoulders by the Creator Himself. However, (as it is in this twenty-first century A.D.) he in no way had dominion over his Creator. This we soon realize because in Genesis 3:1 Adam and Eve meet Lucifer when he comes to poke his nasty nose into the paradise our wonderful God had planted just for them and their offspring (See Ezekiel 28:12-19).

It will be the theme of this writing to show what Lucifer had in his mind as he came to Eden that day. Lucifer did not show up in his true form. He never has since that day, but first came to Eve in the body of a beautiful beast called the serpent. This Verse describes this serpent as the most **subtil** beast of any God had created. **Subtil** (sometimes written subtle) is defined in the *Webster's Dictionary* as: **"thin, not dense or gross; nice; fine; delicate; sly; artful; cunning; crafty; insinuating; deceitful; treacherous."**

Does this definition describe anyone or anything you know? Well, it sure describes the old devil (and a good amount of the media programming presented in the world today) because he is presented to man with all of these attributes and much more. We soon discover this as we read Genesis 3:1b-7, where we find Lucifer's half-truths and whole lies exposed.

> ... And he said unto the woman, Yea, hath God said, Ye shall not eat of **every** tree of the garden? And the woman said unto the serpent, We may eat of the fruit of the **trees** of the garden: But of the fruit of the tree which is in the midst of the garden, God hath said, Ye shall not eat of it, ***neither shall ye touch it,*** lest ye die. And the serpent said unto the woman, Ye shall not surely die: For God doth know that in the day ye eat thereof, then your eyes shall be opened, and ye shall be as gods, knowing good and evil. And when the woman saw that the tree was good for food, and that it was pleasant to the eyes, and a tree to be desired to make one wise, she took of the fruit thereof, and did eat, and gave also unto her husband with her; and he did eat. And the eyes of them both were opened, and they knew that they were naked; and **they sewed fig leaves together,** and made themselves aprons [emphasis mine].

This first act of self-righteousness by Adam and Eve (sewing fig leaves together for a covering) was definitely not recognized by God, as we shall see later. Only the righteousness of God, imputed by God **into** fallen man, will suffice to satisfy our entrance before Him!

I would like to insert here that the whole Bible is a Book about God's relationship with mankind, mankind's relationships with each other, and Lucifer's attempt to destroy both relationships. Genesis 3:1-7 begins that attempt and it will continue until Satan is cast into the lake of fire in Revelation 20:10 after the Millennium.

As we *move* through the remaining Verses of Genesis Chapter 3, we hear God calling Adam in the cool of the day, as He had done before. But Adam does not respond. As God continues to call, Adam finally answers and admits to God he was afraid to answer because he was naked. The Lord God then asks how Adam knew he was naked. *Have you eaten of the tree whereof I commanded you not to eat?* Adam is quick to blame Eve. Eve is quick to blame the devil. In today's world this would be called "passing the buck," but it did not work in the Garden of Eden with our God, and it does not work six thousand years later. Every human being is responsible for their own decisions!

Genesis 3:14–19 then records the **expulsion of this first Adam from the First Eden.** We read:

> And the LORD God said unto the serpent, Because thou hast done this, thou art **cursed above all cattle** [It is at least possible that the serpent was of the "cattle kind" when he appeared to Eve, before he was cursed of God and put upon his belly.], and above every beast of the field; *upon thy belly* shalt thou go, and dust shalt thou eat all the days of thy life: And I will put enmity between thee and the woman, and between thy seed and her seed; **it** [her seed, Jesus Christ] **shall bruise thy head, and thou** [Satan] **shalt bruise his heel.** Unto the woman he said, I will greatly multiply thy sorrow and thy conception; in sorrow thou shalt bring forth children; and thy desire shall be to thy husband, and he shall rule over thee. [Could all births be painless, if Father Adam and Mama Eve had not willfully changed the Words of God and eaten the forbidden fruit?] And unto Adam he said, Because thou hast hearkened unto the voice of thy wife, and hast eaten of the tree, of which I commanded thee, saying,

Thou shalt not eat of it: **cursed** is the ground for thy sake; in sorrow shalt thou eat of it all the days of thy life; Thorns also and thistles shall it bring forth to thee; and **thou shalt eat the herb of the field** [Could we grow crops without weeds if Father Adam had not willfully listened to Mama Eve?]; In the sweat of thy face shalt thou eat bread, till thou return unto the ground [Did Adam sweat before he fell into sin?]; for out of it wast thou taken: for dust thou art, and unto dust shalt thou return [[emphasis and commentary mine].

Just this week I was listening to a world-renowned preacher on TV as he told his large congregation and his world audience how Adam gave this fruit to Eve. It seemed at first to be a verbal error, then it became evident it was an attempt to man-bash Adam—and men in general. I would certainly hope he will soon be made aware of the penalty for misquoting Scripture for personal gain and apologize to God, his congregation, and his world audience. (Read Proverbs 30:5-6).

The Bible makes it very clear that we sin against God because of our will! As it always has been in the past, it was Father Adam's free will to take this forbidden fruit (from his wife) and plunge the human family into sin, degradation, and debauchery. We cannot single out Mother Eve, neither dare we change God's Words concerning this tragic fall of the human family! Adam and Eve had the Words of God and so do we in the received text, underlying the King James Version.

My dear friends: Our life is not a practice run. We had better get it right *in this lifetime!!!* Read Revelation 22:18-19.

As we see this first man and woman about to be **thrust from this first garden paradise in Eden,** we view a loving God slaying animals and making coats of skins to clothe these first two sinners. This covering is a type of the righteousness provided by Jesus Christ and His atoning work four thousand years later on Calvary's cross in the Nation of Israel at Jerusalem.

Also, we hear God proclaiming that the danger of these first two sinners eating of the **tree of life** and living forever in their sin is too great to let them remain in Eden's paradise. It can never be truthfully said that our God is slow at making decisions. God quickly sent them forth from the Garden of Eden, to till the ground from whence they were taken. As we all know (however more effectively he may do it, even calling it no-till in today's modern world), Adam (man) is still tilling the soil of Planet Earth to this very day for his existence!

Note: He (man) will continue to do so until Scriptures like Isaiah 51:3; Ezekiel 34:11-31; 47:1-12; Habakkuk 2:14; 3:3; Zechariah 2:4-13; 14:8-9; Revelation 20:4-6, etc., are fulfilled in our God's final Sabbath—the one thousand-year Holy Millennium.

We watch as God places cherubim and a flaming sword at the east of Eden to guard this tree of life. *Look for this tree of life to show up again in Chapter Eight.* [Note: Cherubim are winged living creatures (see Ezekiel 1:5).]

Thus, this first Dispensation, *Innocence*, where God cared for man personally, comes to a close and man is propelled into the Dispensation of Conscience to fend for himself.

What a sad time this was for those first two humans, and also for the peoples that are about to come on Earth's scene through their future unions.

I truly believe the devil must have been listening very closely when God told him in Genesis 3:15, "And I will put enmity between thee and the woman, and between *thy seed* and *her seed;* it shall bruise thy head, and thou shall bruise his heel." The devil must have had a sense of satisfaction as he watched Adam and Eve leaving the Eden paradise God had planted for them. I believe the devil was planning in his perverted mind a way to destroy this Seed of God that would eventually come from these first two humans to bruise his head. He must have thought that his job would be much easier now.

Over the years of attempting to live for the LORD, I have come to understand one thing: The devil is smart like a fox in some ways, and dumb as a box of rocks in other ways! **Smart** in the fact he learned very early how to appeal to the fleshly side of Adam's family. It worked for him in the Garden of Eden, and it is still working today. I believe the devil thought if he could get Adam and Eve on the **outside of this protective paradise**, he could work his havoc in the human family and stop his head-bruising in the future.

On the other hand, he is ***dumb*** enough to fight against the omnipotent God of the universe. He evidently thinks that eventually he can win and overpower God. However, as we *move* **Beyond the Revelation** to Chapter 20:1-3, God lets us know of his future holding place for one thousand years. After the thousand years are expired, he must be loosed for a little season, to deceive those living during the Millennium who were not serious about their relationship with the King, Jesus Christ. Then (as noted before), he will be cast into the lake of fire for all eternity (Revelation 20:10). **Hallelujah—no more devil!**

As we go to our next Chapters, we must remember that the Adam family has now been **cast from the First Eden** and has begun the long and painful wait before he will be permitted to **enter The Last Eden.** If God keeps His Biblical mandate of six being the number of man and seven being the number of divine completeness, then we should expect between these two Edens approximately six thousand years (six God days) of misery and mayhem, with the joy of God's grace sprinkled along the way, before day seven: the Holy Day of the Lord's Millennium rest for Planet Earth. During these six thousand years, our God will be working with all mankind to bring him to the knowledge of the truth. Without this sprinkling of the grace of a loving God, no doubt the same Satan who first appeared to Eve in the First Eden would consume the human family. If this were accomplished, everything God set forth in Genesis 1–3 would be eternally lost!

As we make our *journey* through Scripture to get to **The Last Eden,** we will see Satan attempt to overthrow this promise made in Genesis 3:15 many times. Pay close attention *as we travel from The First Eden to The Last Eden,* keeping in mind what old Satan has up his sleeve!

However, God's eye is on the sparrow, His eye was on this "promised Seed," and His eye is on you and me. **Praise His Holy Name!**

Beloved, be aware that God's Holy eye is on us, even at this very moment. Listen as 1 Thessalonians 5:23 gives encouragement with these Words: "And the very God of peace **sanctify you wholly;** and I pray God your whole **spirit** and **soul** and **body** be preserved blameless unto the coming of our Lord Jesus Christ." In this blessed Scriptural promise, our God is also making us aware that man is a trinity, just as God is a Trinity. In this one manner, we (mankind) truly are created in the image of God. This is a fact the devil has hated from day one and he (as we have already stated) will attempt to destroy **the genetic makeup of man** that he may prevent the birth of the second Adam in Bethlehem Ephratah. If he can accomplish this feat, he will inevitably stop his head-bruising at Calvary, as he was promised in Genesis 3:15. Realizing this, it is possible Genesis 3:15 could be the most relevant Scripture in all of God's Holy Bible!

May I now say that without Genesis 3:15 being fulfilled at Calvary, all of mankind would have been lost and there would have been **NO LAST EDEN!**

As we are about to leave this Chapter, Lucifer no doubt thinks he is well on his way to accomplishing his dirty feat as he observes Adam and Eve leaving this paradise of protection, **the First Eden.** But, as we will see, God *moved,* Joseph waited, Mary believed, and Jesus was born! HOLY, HOLY, HOLY IS HIS NAME!

Read Luke 3:23-38 for the full genealogy of Mary listed through Heli, her father-in-law. Joseph was begotten of Jacob, his father, in Matthew 1:16.

Now, we will *move* on to Chapter Two and start our *journey.*

Chapter Two

The Journey Begins

As we start our *journey* in Chapter Two, my mind goes back to my early years on the farm in Middle Tennessee. It is almost impossible for me to comprehend the changes that have occurred in tilling the soil of Planet Earth in my lifetime. I am convinced that in my early childhood not much had improved in this tilling process since the days of Adam and his offspring, even though Genesis 4:16–24 suggests that about one hundred twenty–eight years after Cain's birth, the Cainitic civilization had become much more advanced after Cain made a move to Nod on the east of Eden. There will be more on this subject as our *journey* through Scripture resumes later.

In 1950 my family also made a *move*—not to Nod on the east end of Eden, but to Pappy's farm on the east end of Lox Creek. We made this *move* in order to live with Mammy and take care of her after Pappy had suddenly died from heart failure. Please believe me when I say this *move* had nothing to do with Eden.

As a seven–year–old boy, my lifestyle of relative ease (notice I said relative ease) was about to turn into a much different lifestyle, one of constant chores and plain hard work! You might be asking yourself about now how much hard work would or could a seven–year–old boy do? Well, in those days, my Dad had what might be described as the perfect poverty program: **we all worked!** Everyone in the family had their own job to do, and we did it. Period!

After the *move,* my Dad had much better conditions for farming. He used mules (Ole John, Ole Blue, and Miss Idder) to pull farming implements, which consisted mostly of what belonged to my Pappy's estate. These implements (which were pulled by mules) included:

1. a very heavy 250-pound Syracuse flip-wing **turning plow** to break up the soil on the steep hillsides;
2. a **drag-harrow** (for leveling down the plowed soil) which was homemade by mounting two large square timbers (approximately ten inches by ten inches by eight feet long) in a "v" with the point of the "v" turned to the front. Dad then took a brace-and-bit and hand-bored holes in the center of the timbers at strategic points down each side of this large "v." He then drove in prepared steel pins (approximately one inch square) into these holes to the proper depth. Lastly, he mounted a steel plate with holes across the front, in which could be inserted a clevis and pin for the single-tree. Chains coming from the mule's britches would be hooked to each end of the single-tree to pull the drag-harrow. (The point for this extended explanation being, in those days if you didn't have it, *sometimes* you made it. I feel this is exactly what Adam must have done in his day);
3. a **bull-tongue plow** to prepare the rows before planting;
4. a **one-row corn planter** that ran in the furrow that the bull-tongue plow had prepared;
5. a **double-shovel plow** used for tilling the crops during growing season;
6. a **gee-whiz** (multiple tooth plow) used for extreme conditions when it rained too much in early spring and made

the grass and weeds grow thick;
7. a **mowing machine** used for cutting hay (five-foot swath);
8. a **rake** used for raking the hay into long windrows which would later be pulled into shocks (by hand);
9. a **slide** used for gathering corn (by hand) on the steep hillsides where a wagon could not sit upright. This slide was made on the farm by my Dad from components taken from the available wood on hand. The runners were made from small logs, hand-hewn, with steel from the outside rim of a buggy wheel that had been disassembled and flattened. The hardened steel from the buggy wheel would then be bolted under the bottom of these log runners to prevent the runners from wearing down when pulled across the ground. The bed, sideboards, and tailgate were made from lumber coming from whatever source Dad had available at the time. Believe it or not, this homemade slide was one of the most used of all the farm implements. It could be pulled with one mule and maneuvered in hard-to-reach places much better than a larger wagon. You could say it was the four-wheel-drive of its day!
10. a **wagon** on which hay would be loaded (by hand). This wagon served two functions: it served as a hay wagon if you put the hay flat on with standards. These standards were long poles that stuck up around the flat to hold the hay from sliding during transport. It also served as a grain wagon if you mounted the grain bed, which had a solid bottom with solid sides.

I remember one time my Dad was taking corn for stone grinding at the water powered mill about five miles from the farm. He had to travel over a dirt and gravel road that was worn full of potholes. Dad warned me that I did not need to go on this long trip, but I was not about to miss a trip to town. By the time we got back to Lox Creek, I thought my bones in my legs and feet had been driven up through my body! This was one of my many experiences in learning that **father knows best!**

This wagon was very similar to the wagons used by those who settled our great country in earlier times. Its wheels had heavy steel bands around wooden spokes with a non-bearing hub. The hub was mounted on a tapered spindle made of hardened steel. When the spindle was properly greased (which had to be done often), the hub literally floated on grease. Most of the wagon's frame was wood with very few steel components.

Would Adam have used a wagon and other implements similar to what Dad used in the late 1940s? (See Genesis 4:16-22.)

I remember my Dad knew just the right way to place the hay on the hay-flat with his pitchfork so as to make it easy to unload at the barn with the hayfork that came down from the highest point in the loft. This unloading system was also pulled by a mule and was a sight to watch while in motion. It was a mechanism of pulleys through which a long, large, cotton rope was attached to a sharp steel spear that would trip when activated by a pull rope. This large steel spear was equipped with an internal trigger, which would move out into the hay when activated at the wagon. Once the hay was pulled up to the steel rail in the top of the barn, it then could move from one end of the barn to the other. Being the only male child in this farm family, I was nominated to lead Ole Blue, as he was the one mule that knew how to pull the hayfork lift. You see, if the mule didn't stop when Dad tripped the load of hay off the hayfork into the loft of the barn, he would very likely pull the whole system out the end of the barn. I was always terrified that Ole Blue would step on my feet or, even worse, not stop. Well, Ole Blue never did either one. I have often thought, in later years of my life, that this hybrid creature was given more than a mule's share of brains. I believe his intelligence was sent from God to bless one very young country boy and his family during very difficult times.

In those days, we cut most of our wood with a double-bitted chopping axe and a crosscut saw. I remember my Dad would go to the wooded hillsides and find fallen trees (good and dry) to cut wood for the cook stove. After dragging these prepared tree sections to the house with Ole Blue, who always seemed to know the way to the barn, especially if it was close to feeding time. Dad would then cut the wood into short lengths and split them into very small pieces to fit the firebox of a large Enterprise cook stove in my Mammy's kitchen.

Ladies, just imagine cooking dinner on this wood-burning stove during a hot August day inside of a very small kitchen with no fan or ventilation. It was very toasty on a cold winter day, but summer was a different story!

In those days, I don't remember if Mom's deodorant failed, and it might be because I don't remember her having deodorant. In fact, I don't remember anyone having deodorant. I have seen my Mom come out of the kitchen as wet as if she had been dunked in the river, but I don't remember hearing her complain. In those days it was not a sin to be poor; however, it was an abomination to be unthankful!

Well, anyway, the cook stove was nice, with its large hot water tank on the right hand side and the warmer boxes up over the top. In those days, hot water was a premium for washing dishes in the dishpan and, also, for washing me, too, even if I did have to be washed in a wash pan with a washcloth!

My Mom made her own soap out of meat skins, lye, and water. We killed our own hogs for meat, and Mom would save the salt-cured meat skins and trimmings used during the months, then put them in the large black kettle, add the right amount of water, and boil them for a long time over a hot fire.

Then she would remove the skins and add the lye (she knew just how much to put in). Afterward, she would cook this concoction until it thickened. When it cooled, she would take the butcher knife and cut the soap into bars. I have watched as my Momma's hands bled from rubbing clothes on a rub-board in the winter months, as she washed clothes in a #4 washtub, using this lye soap. If your clothes survived the boiling water and this lye soap, they would usually be *clean.* The lye may have been a little hard on the skin when you sweated during the summer, but you had clean clothes!

I cannot help but wonder how Adam and Eve did their washing in 4004 B.C. after God removed them from the Garden of Eden. Did Eve have a #4 washtub like my Momma? I guess we will have to wait and ask her later.

I remember one particular time at our second home (when I was about four or five years old) my Mom was washing on her rub-board on our small back porch. As she went up and down, my pet goat, Browney, saw the up and down movement of Mom's lower backside. Well, to a pet goat that had gotten old enough to feel his goat hormones, this was too much to resist! He came charging to Mom with horns cocked and almost butted her over into the washtub. If you had known my Momma, I would not need to tell you what happened next, but since you never met her I will go on and explain. Mom grabbed the broom and beat Browney up *good.* You see, Browney was a nervous goat, and when he got scared, he fainted. This was bad news for Mom's broom—and for poor Browney. As I remember, a few weeks later Browney ate the sleeves off my Dad's **only** white Sunday shirt, which was hanging outside on the clothesline to dry. Mr. Browney was sold to the cattle trader the next day for three dollars. Since he belonged to me, Mom gave me the money. I remember thinking I must be rich with three dollars in my bank. This was probably the first time

I had ever held a dollar bill in my hand, because up until this goat deal, I only got small change from finding hens' nests on the hills around our house and barn. I would then trade these eggs to the peddler for this small change, which went back to the peddler for candy.

Also at Mammy's house we had to carry, in buckets, all our water from a spring up in the holler. This is one of the many chores I previously referred to.

Oh, yes! Our toilet was on the outside of the house and it was air-conditioned, especially in the winter months. Our toilet tissue came from the mailbox in the form of a Sears-Roebuck catalogue (last year's issue), which we would wad up to cause wrinkles in the paper for better results. You understand, don't you?

Needless to say, after the *move* to Mammy's on the east end of Lox Creek, I really missed the running water that came from the cave, the indoor toilets, the drop-in water heater, and large bathtub at Aunt Callie's rent house. Surely, you can understand why!

The good news is, after two years at Mammy's, she decided to *move* in with one of Dad's brothers and sell the farm. Guess where our next *move* was to be? You got it right. Dad rented Aunt Callie's hillside farm.

Happy days were here, again on Lox Creek!

It really would be interesting to know what kind of facilities and tools these first farmers used after their expulsion from Eden, because we read in Genesis 4:1-2 that Adam and Eve bore two sons: Cain and Abel. These Scriptures tell us that Abel was a keeper of sheep and Cain was a tiller of the soil. I would think Cain had some form of implements, as Genesis 4:3 tells us that **in process of time**, Cain brought of the fruit of the ground an offering unto the Lord.

Also, we read in Genesis 4:22a: "And Zillah, she also bare

Tubal-cain, an instructer of every **artificer in brass and iron.**" *Artificer* is defined in my Old *Webster's Dictionary* as "a skilled craftsman, one who invents, one whose occupation requires skill or knowledge of a particular kind."

As mentioned before, the listing of time chronology by James Ussher places this Tubal-cain one hundred twenty-eight years after the birth of Cain, the first son of Adam and Eve. Keeping this one hundred twenty-eight-year span in mind, I realized it has only been fifty-nine years since my Daddy plowed with a mule and planted corn with a one-row planter and harvested *all* of his crops by hand.

How do you think my Dad's farming practices would compare with those who till the soil in 2009?

I was recently in West Tennessee at a Christian brother's farm and saw his new John Deere four-wheel-drive combine. It had numerous onboard computers (five in all) to control each function of this massive wonder, with its ability to cut, harvest, and clean a thirty-foot swath of grain at one pass. When I stepped back and looked at the tremendous size of this monster machine, I was made to wonder just how the transport trucks hauled it on the two-lane roads of West Tennessee. This Christian brother also uses massive four-wheel-drive tractors to pull a sixteen-row grain-planter that is forty-two feet wide, and a grain drill (for soybeans and wheat) that will plant a swath forty-five feet wide. These massive tractors also have onboard auto-steer GPS systems which steer them from one end of a field to the other and they will not be off track more than four inches.

Weeds, grass, and thistles will not have much of a chance to choke the crops anymore (as they did fifty-nine years ago in my childhood) because in the place of a gooseneck hoe (with the handle cut off) like I had to use in Pappy's hillside field, this brother is using a giant self-propelled sprayer spraying a whopping eighty-foot swath of chemicals over the top of these growing plants in his thousands-of-acres, round-up-ready, no-till operation.

If the farming practices of Tubal-cain advanced in the one hundred twenty-eight years from his father, Adam, until his mention in Scripture as much as men have advanced in the last fifty-nine years since my childhood when Daddy pulled his plow with a mule, Cain and his descendants' ability to till the soil could have been tremendous.

How sad that we who are Christians will probably never be able to ask Cain about this matter because in his self-righteous act of bringing the works of his hands for a sacrificial offering, he was rejected by God and eventually slew Abel his brother (read Genesis 4:5 and 1 John 3:12). However, Abel was accepted because Abel brought a **blood sacrifice** of the firstlings of his flock to offer to the Lord (read Genesis 4:4). In 4004 B.C., it took **blood** to satisfy the demand of the Lord, and nothing has changed.

Many of the religions in America and the nations of the world have censored the blood from all segments of religious life. However, God is the same yesterday, today, and forever, and changeth not! Christ's atoning work on the cross at Calvary is still the **all-sufficient payment for the sins of the human family.** That payment was God's blood. Those who censor the blood-atoning power of Jesus Christ from their plan of redemption will reap the same reward Cain received in the beginning of human history.

Some folks may have forgotten that no payment is final until it is applied to the debt. Please take a few minutes and examine yourself and see if your sin-debt is free and clear. It will make all the difference when you arrive in eternity if God's blood has been applied to your soul (Spiritually) by grace through faith in Jesus Christ. Please make sure you don't wind up like Cain! God will let the believer in Christ know things are right in their soul by supplying **permanent peace within!** AMEN.

In this sin-charged atmosphere of 4004 B.C. we read of God once again blessing Adam and Eve with a son, whom Eve named Seth (meaning substituted or appointed). Remember, wicked Cain had slain Abel, his first brother.

In process of time to Seth was born a son, and he called his name Enos. After the birth of Enos, the Bible tells us in Genesis 4:26 that men began to call on the name of the Lord. This is very important to note as we *travel on our journey* through early civilization to go **Beyond the Revelation to The Last Eden.**

In Chapter Five of Genesis the Scriptures take off like a rocket ship, and forty Verses later (in Genesis 6:7) we have arrived to a time in human history when the world is facing total destruction by a global flood. At first glance, one might feel these forty Verses are just coincidence, but maybe not.

In his tremendous book *God the Master Mathematician,* Noah Hutchings tells us that **forty is the number of testing.** On page 107 of his book, he reminds us this number is first used in Genesis 7:4. We read: "For yet seven days, and I will cause it to rain upon the earth **forty days** and **forty nights;** and every living substance that I have made will I destroy from off the face of the earth."

What could have possibly happened in the mind of God to prompt Him to use only **forty Verses of Scripture** (Genesis 4:26-6:7) to span sixteen hundred and fifty-one years of time from the birth of Seth to the announcement that He would bring about a worldwide destruction by water of **all** human, animal, fowl, insect, or any other life form that did not come into the ark or swim in water? Why does God's Word have a certain mystical silence about sixteen hundred and fifty-one years of human history in Scripture? Has something happened in this human family so horrendous that our God had just as soon not talk about it in His Holy Word? Let's look farther and see.

We take note in Genesis 5, the lineage through Seth is given down to Noah and Genesis 6:8-9 may give us the reason why God has put the Scriptures into overdrive. We read: "**But Noah found grace in the eyes of the Lord.** These are the generations of Noah: Noah was **a just man** and **perfect in his generations,** and Noah walked with God."

Just who are the generations that preceded Noah through Seth? Let's read in Genesis Chapters 5-9 and see.

- Adam begat Seth and lived a total of 930 years—Genesis 5:5
- Seth begat Enos and lived a total of 912 years—Genesis 5:8
- Enos begat Cainan and lived a total of 905 years—Genesis 5:11
- Cainan begat Mahalaleel and lived a total of 910 years—Genesis 5:14
- Mahalaleel begat Jared and lived a total of 895 years—Genesis 5:17
- Jared begat Enoch and lived a total of 962 years—Genesis 5:20
- Enoch begat Methuselah and lived a total of 365 years, "for God took him"—Genesis 5:23-24
- Methuselah begat Lamech and lived a total of 969 years—Genesis 5:27
- Lamech begat Noah and lived a total of 777 years—Genesis 5:31
- Noah begat Shem, Ham, and Japheth and lived 950 years—Genesis 9:29 [Note: Noah begat Shem, Ham, and Japheth after age five hundred (Genesis 5:32). He was in his six hundredth year when the flood came. He lived three hundred

and fifty years after the flood. Total 950 years.]

On page 92 of his book *God the Master Mathematician*, Dr. Noah Hutchings also lets us know that **ten** is the number in Scripture that signifies completion of God's divine order: Noah was the tenth generation from Adam, which completed the Antediluvian civilization.

Remembering that Genesis 6:9 tells us that Noah was perfect in his generations, we will now look at the definition of generations. The Hebrew word for "generations" is *tol-dah*. The definition of *tol-dah* in *Strong's Hebrew Exhaustive Concordance of the Old Testament* is, **descent, family, history, birth.**

The 1828 edition of the *Webster's Dictionary of the English Language* gives us basically the same definition for the English word "generations." It reads: "Genealogy; a series of children or descendants **from the same stock.**" I feel these definitions of generations are very important because this lets us know Noah had the same genes (or stock) as did his father, Adam. Adam was made "fresh" from the hands of our loving God.

Is this **gene factor** coupled with **God's righteousness** the reason God used this man Noah (and seven family members) to bring the human family **through** the universal flood and eventually repopulate Planet Earth? Read Genesis 6:8–9 again! Remember, God originally populated Planet Earth with just two people, Adam and Eve. This time He is using eight people because eight is the number in the Scriptures for beginning again or new beginnings.

Also, the question is looming in Scripture: What happened to all of Earth's population (except eight souls) in this sixteen hundred and fifty-one year span from Genesis 4:26 to Genesis 6:7? Had Satan raised his dastardly head to do his dirty work again, as he did in the Garden of Eden? Is he remembering the promise of a head-bruising? You see, my friend, Satan is a loser, but as we would say in the hill country of Middle Tennessee, he's a *mean, dirty, lousy loser,* never giving up without a fight to the end!

We will attempt to show as we *move forward* that Satan has not forgotten Genesis 3:15 for one minute as he works his havoc in this blessed human family that has been created in the image of our Holy God to bring Him glory on Planet Earth. The events coming up in Chapter Three should not surprise anyone who is acquainted with Satan's wicked and abominable ways. Let's face it. There is nothing Satan will not do to get back at his creator for booting him from his position as archangel in God's heavenly realm.

(Note: Definition of **archangel**: An angel of the highest order; an angel occupying the "eighth rank" in the celestial order.)

Listen to the language of God's Word as He goes beyond this earthly king of Babylon in a parade of "I wills" to describe Lucifer in Isaiah 14:12-17.

> How art thou **fallen from heaven, O Lucifer, son of the morning!** how art thou cut down to the ground, which didst weaken the nations! For thou hast said in thine heart, **I will** ascend into heaven, **I will** exalt my throne above the stars of God: **I will** sit also upon the mount of the congregation, in the sides of the north: **I will** ascend above the heights of the clouds; **I will** be like the most High. **Yet thou shalt be brought down to hell,** to the sides of the pit. They that see thee shall narrowly look upon thee, and consider thee, saying, Is this the man that made the earth to tremble, that did shake kingdoms; That made the world as a wilderness, and destroyed the cities thereof; that opened not the house of his prisoners? [emphasis mine]

In like manner, the Word of God truly goes beyond this earthly king of Tyrus to describe Lucifer in Ezekiel 28:12-16.

> Son of man, take up a lamentation upon the king of Tyrus, and say unto him, Thus saith the Lord GOD; Thou sealest up the sum, full of wisdom, and **perfect in beauty. Thou hast been in Eden the garden of God;** every precious stone was thy covering, the sardius, topaz, and the diamond, the beryl, the onyx, and the jasper, the sapphire, the emerald, and the carbuncle, and gold: the workmanship of thy tabrets and of thy pipes was prepared in thee in the day **that thou wast created.** Thou art the **anointed cherub** that covereth; and I have set thee so: **thou wast upon the holy mountain of God;** thou hast walked up and down in the midst of the stones of fire. **Thou wast perfect in thy ways from the day that thou wast created, till iniquity was found in thee.** By the multitude of thy merchandise they have filled the midst of thee with violence, and thou hast sinned: therefore I will cast thee as profane out of the mountain of God: and I will destroy thee, **O covering cherub,** from the midst of the stones of fire" [emphasis mine].

I would not think anyone would believe that the king of Babylon (712 B.C.) was at any time in Heaven with our Holy God, nor did he bear the name "son of the morning." These are attributes of Lucifer in his beauty before and after his fall (Isaiah 14:12; Ezekiel 28:14-15)! Neither would I think the king of Tyrus (588 B.C.) was perfect in beauty and visited Eden, the garden of God (Ezekiel 28:12-13). Also, I would never believe either of these earthly kings was anointed cherubs, because Ezekiel 1 and 10 lets us know that cherubs are winged creatures (angels) that minister to God. This was Lucifer's archangel position until pride caused his fall.

We will now *move on* to Chapter Three in our *journey* to go **Beyond the Revelation.**

We will begin at Genesis 6:1-7 in the Holy Scriptures and also use some historical accounts to possibly help us understand just what happened in this most awful time in human history. We must remember that most of the bad things recorded in past history are a direct result of the devil trying to overthrow the plan and purpose of our Holy God and **stop the advancement of the promised Seed through which would be born the Messiah, Jesus Christ!**

As Christians, we would do well to **watch** for this fallen angel deceiver in every aspect of human living in these last days of apostasy and mayhem! Satan is definitely not looking forward to his **continued head-bruising,** thus he will attempt to stop these prophesied events any way possible! This would include installing a one-man world ruler on the throne of David in Jerusalem (see Daniel 9:27; 11:31,45; Matthew 24:15).

Remember Mark 13:37: "And what I say unto you I say unto all, **Watch.**"

Remember: Failure to heed the prophets of God has brought down every nation in history who chose such a path!

Chapter Three

Look Dad, There's Giants Out There

As a young child, I well remember the first time I saw Superman flying through the skies with his cape waving in the rushing wind. I also remember the sounds and sights that to a young hillbilly boy (who had not been off his home turf many times) seemed so real. I soon became convinced men could fly! I'll give you one guess where I saw him. You got it right, on Uncle John's black and white TV in the 1950s. If my memory serves me correctly, Superman was supposed to have **come down to Earth from the Planet Krypton** with super strength and abilities no human on Earth possessed. Even back then humanity was looking for a superhuman to come to Earth that could cure all their problems. As a child I would wonder how you could kill a man and him not remain dead (read Revelation 13:3,12-14).

Also as a child, I had no idea what the cartoon world would become in my lifetime. Today, as Satan prepares the world for Antichrist, we have a satanic maze of devil-oriented characters gradually destroying the very moral fiber of American life. In this maze of the cartoon and media world in general, you can find anything from graphic sex to blatant sorcery.

Many American Christians are letting their children and

themselves soak it in like sponges in vinegar. As you travel the cartoon gambit, you will also find murder, witchcraft, sodomy, violence, and cursing, to mention a few malignancies. This is corruption of kids in every respect. Some of the monsters in today's cartoon world and in Hollywood no doubt resemble the giants and mighty men of renown mentioned in Genesis 6:4.

The next question we should ask ourselves is: Where on Earth did these **giants** listed in Genesis 6:4 originate?

Was Adam a giant? Was Eve a giant? As you know, she was taken out of Adam's side. We know that Adam and Eve produced children after their kind with good genes. So, the question remains: What happened?

Realizing that Satan has been the culprit in causing Adam and Eve to *be moved* outside of Eden, we cannot help but wonder what he has pulled out of his sleeve in his quest to **outdo** our holy God and **undo** Genesis 3:15, Romans 16:20, and Revelation 20:10?

Let's review his promised head-bruising in these three Scriptural Verses to help keep us up to date on what Satan might be up to!

» Genesis 3:15—"And I will put enmity between thee and the woman, and between thy seed and her seed; it shall **bruise** thy head, and thou shalt bruise his heel."
» Romans 16:20—"And the God of peace shall **bruise** Satan under your feet shortly. [Read 1 Corinthians 6:3; Daniel 7:22,27.] The grace of our Lord Jesus Christ be with you. Amen."
» Revelation 20:10—"And the devil that deceived them was cast into the lake of fire and brimstone, where the beast and the false prophet **are** [after one thousand years], and shall be **tormented** day and night for ever and ever."

With these three Verses digested, let's get back to the giants.

For sure, we know these giants did not come from the same seed as Noah because Noah was perfect in his generations (Genesis 6:9). Noah walked with God, preached righteous preaching (2 Peter 2:5), was delivered through the flood, and took part in the repopulation of the Earth in post-flood days (Genesis 8:16-17). To say the least, Noah had good **genes** (**seed**) and was right with God at this time (read Genesis 9:1,9; Hebrews 11:7).

Also, we know when God created every living thing, He made them to reproduce **after their kind.** One thing is for sure: these giants are not the same *"kind"* as Noah and his offspring!

Stanley E. Price in *The Giants of Noah's Day* quotes the **Companion Bible's** footnotes to Genesis 6:9:

> The Hebrew word *tamin* means "without blemish" and is the technical word for bodily physical perfection and not moral. Hence, it is used of animals and sacrificial "purity." It is rendered "without blemish" in Exodus 12:5, 29:1; Leviticus 1:3 (and a host of other Scriptures too numerous to mention)....This shows Genesis 6:9 does not speak of Noah's moral perfection, but, tells us he...alone had preserved the pedigree, keeping it pure, in spite of prevailing corruption brought about by the fallen angels cohabiting with the daughters of men.

Well, we can also rule out "righteous" women marrying unrighteous men (godly Sethites marrying ungodly Cainites), as my reference Bible suggests in the footnotes. I have used this particular reference Bible since the time I was first saved; however, the footnotes of this Bible (or any other Bible) are not divinely inspired. Only the text of God's preserved Word is inspired by God. I know of numbers of godly men and women marrying ungodly mates, but I have not seen a single giant in Middle Tennessee in my lifetime! Extra large, healthy hillbillies, sure; giants, no!

However, unless we are raptured pretty soon, I suppose we will see giants on the Earth again, because the Scriptures plainly teach: **"But as the days of Noe were, so shall also the coming of the Son of man be"** (Matthew 24:37).

I was recently told of identical twins that are between seven and eight feet tall coming out of the country of China. There is speculation that they may be clones. I remembered I had seen one of these individuals on the TV as he was involved in some kind of sport, possibly basketball.

In this mixed up world in which we live, we sometimes want to ask: Does a human clone have a soul? Can these clones be saved? Will clones grow to the proper size, or when scientists mess with human genes will they grow to be giants? Did the men before the flood mess with the gene–pool or DNA as we are doing? Who is capable of giving us the answer to these and other questions? Has over one hundred years of Darwinian theology finally convinced a majority of the human family that we are nothing but common animals?

In his tremendous book *Introduction to Theology,* page 371, Dr. Harold Willmington gives us this insight. After listing his first two views, he writes:

> **In conclusion: it should be noted that a third view has been recently advocated which says the sons of God were indeed fallen angels who totally controlled and possessed all the evil men living before the flood. These demons may have even attempted to change (by genetic engineering, as we see today) the DNA code of future babies like some deadly virus.**

Well, we know for sure something happened to change the genetic structuring of the human family, because before the flood of Noah's day there was a world of perverted people our God could not reach, even with one hundred twenty years of preaching from His man, Noah.

It would seem they were so evil our Holy God had very little to say about the matter in the short forty verses (sixteen hundred and fifty-one years) covering this period from the birth of Enos in Genesis 4:26 to the pronouncement of universal judgment over the whole earth in Genesis 6:7. Do you believe it would be appropriate to ask, **WHY?** (One hundred twenty years of godly preaching with no conversions is totally unthinkable to me.)

We will now read Genesis 6:1-7,12-13, and look farther into this genetic dilemma. Remembering Genesis 3:15, we can be sure that Satan will have his finger in the pie:

> And it came to pass, when men began to multiply on the face of the earth, and daughters were born unto them, **That the sons of God saw the daughters of men** that they were fair; and **they took them wives of all which they chose.** And the LORD said, My spirit shall not always strive with man, for that he also is flesh: yet his days shall be an hundred and twenty years. **There were giants in the earth in those days; and also after that, when the sons of God came in unto the daughters of men, and they bare children to them, the same became mighty men which were of old, men of renown.** And GOD saw that the wickedness of man was great in the earth, and that **every imagination of the thoughts of his heart was only evil continually.** And it re-**pented the LORD** that he had made man on the earth, and **it grieved him at his heart.** And the LORD said, I will destroy man whom I have created from the face of the earth; both

man, and beast, and the creeping thing, and the fowls of the air; for **it repenteth me** that I have made **them**.... And God looked upon the earth, and, behold, it was corrupt; for **all flesh had corrupted his way** upon the earth. And God said unto Noah, **The end of all flesh is come before me;** for the earth is filled with violence **through *them***; and, behold, I will **destroy *them* with the earth** [emphasis mine].

Wow! What has happened to the human family, causing a holy and loving God to make these statements? Was it really a complete DNA change over many decades in the whole human family? Was it so bad God calls what He created in His image "them"? Were these Antediluvian people products of fallen angels who are now kept in chains under darkness, who kept not their first estate, but left their own habitation, marrying human women (read Genesis 6:2; 2 Peter 2:4; Jude 6)?

Listen as we review how God speaks to these perverse *Antediluvians:*

» My spirit shall not always strive with **man**
» His days shall be **an hundred and twenty years**
» And **it repented the LORD** that he had made man on the earth
» I will **destroy man** whom I have created from the face of the earth
» **All flesh** had corrupted his way upon the earth
» I will **destroy them** with the earth.

Who on earth is **"them"**? Is it those to whom Noah preached one hundred twenty years with no recorded converts (see Genesis 6:3–4,12–13)?

Note: Is this the same God of love speaking who we see coming down from the Third Heaven and walking in the cool of the day, talking with Adam and Eve in the First Eden?

Is this the same God of love speaking who sought out Adam and Eve after they had sinned by eating the forbidden fruit?

Is this the same God of love speaking who slew animals to make clothing for both of these sinners as they were being expelled from Eden, showing His forgiveness of their sin, and also pointing them toward Calvary, when Jesus would die for **all** the sins of the world?

Is this the same God of love speaking who said to wicked Cain in Genesis 4:7a, "If thou doest well, shalt thou not be accepted? . . ."

Is this the same God of love speaking who is calling today **whosoever will** to come to repentance and faith and live eternally with Him?

The answer is an emphatic "YES!" However, with this group of people in Genesis 6:1–7, 10–13, our God is showing no mercy! I do not know what was going through the mind of God at this time, but I do know it was not good as far as this race of giants and mighty men of renown were concerned. Something *beyond all human comprehension* had transpired in the human family; thus, our God *was not* going to have anything to do with it. **Period!**

If this had just been sinful men marrying righteous women, or righteous men marrying sinful women, would God have had such an unforgiving, blatant attitude toward them? I don't think so. Do you? He cleansed and forgave Adam and Eve as sinners. He cleansed and saved me from my sins. I believe if God would save me, He would save anyone who would repent and turn to Him. However, the question is looming: Had these perverted Antediluvians already passed God's deadline and become reprobates?

Do we believe anyone from this group of giants would have provided a suitable future seed from which the virgin

Mary could be born? The virgin Mary was born of the seed of Shem, through Abraham, through David, to become the human mother of Jesus Christ, God's Holy Son! In the New Testament Gospels, we hear Jesus called, "the Son of David" numerous times. We must remember that God, the Holy Ghost, spiritually overshadowed this young virgin who conceived and bore the Only Begotten Son of God. He was the son of David naturally! Thus, Jesus Christ became God incarnate!

Was the Old Testament prophecy of Christ being born of the seed of David the source of what God was considering *2353*[10] *years into the future* as He makes these grave pronouncements on these perverse Antediluvians?

Was God also keeping the promise He made in Genesis 3:15 concerning Satan's head being bruised at Calvary? It would seem to me He is considering all of the aforementioned promises, and more!

As we continue Chapter Three, we will farther examine this genetic dilemma referencing the best sources available on this subject.

In his book, *The Giants of Noah's Day,* Brother Stanley E. Price has compiled both his work and Dr. Noah Hutchings work on this subject of the Antediluvian civilization. These brothers have, by far, the best sources I have read on this matter. We will use (by permission) some of their labors, and others, in an attempt to better provide the answer to our questions.

On page four and five of this tremendous work, Brother Price gives us this information on the modern interpretation written by Matthew Henry (copyright 1961) as follows: "The sons of Seth (that is the professors of religion) married the daughters of men (that is those who were profane and strangers to God and godliness). The posterity of Seth did not keep

---

10. Ussher, *Annals of the World*

by themselves, as they ought to have done. They intermingled with the excommunicated race of Cain."

However, as it is noted on page five, this is totally the conclusion of the writer. Nowhere in the Bible does it even infer that the "sons of God" were men from the line of Seth and the "daughters of men" were the women from the line of Cain. All *from both lines* were destroyed in the flood with the exception of Noah and his household. Both the lineage of Seth and the lineage of Cain were judged **equally** by God [emphasis mine].

In his book, *Satan: The Prince of Darkness*, Frederick A. Tatford says:

> It was Satan's purpose ... to contaminate the whole Adamic womanhood and thereby **to prevent the advent of the promised seed.** ... Angelic beings voluntarily left their aerial habitation and surrendered their dignities and responsibilities in order to commit the impious outrage of **cohabiting with Adam's descendants.** Using their inherent **power of materialization,** they entered into **incongruous union** with women on earth, the offspring of these unnatural marriages being the heroes who were of old, men of renown.

Note: This question of angelic materialization (fallen angelical spirits appearing in human form) was mentioned in a Bible study I was teaching recently, and at that time I was of the opinion these fallen angels simply entered into humans (that had been born of women) and polluted their being. However, after a more in-depth study of Genesis 18-19; John 20:11-12; Mark 16:5; Luke 1:26-38, 2:8-15, 24:4; Genesis 32:1-2; Joshua 5:13-15; Hebrews13:1, and a host of other Scriptures, it has become overwhelmingly evident, at least to my understanding, angels do indeed materialize on Planet Earth. As far as I can understand, none of these Scriptures mentioned insinuate these are angel incarnates. There are men and women in this present world who are, no doubt, possessed by demonic spirits. Yet, as far as I know, they do not bear giants when they conceive children. As hillbilly folks say: *Let's just shell down the corn and face the truth: Ten feet tall men and women with up to a twenty-two-inch foot span are not natural!*

These unnatural genes would account for the unnatural characteristics of these giants. In post-flood times, Deuteronomy 3:11 records one such giant, **Og** by name, having a bedstead of iron which was nine cubits in length and four cubits in width. These cubits are defined in the center column reference of my Bible as 1'5.48" or 17.48". Believing these references to be correct, let's do the math. 17.48" × 9 cubit =157.32" ÷ 12" = a 13'11" long bed; 17.48" × 4 cubit = 69.92" ÷ 12" = a 5'9" wide bed. **May I now say, a 13'11" × 5'9" bed, even in hillbilly terms is a whopper!!!** However, a footnote in the book by Josephus, *Antiquities of the Jews*, gives a cubit as 21 English inches. 21 × 9 = 189"; 189 ÷ 12" = 15'9" long bed. 21 × 4 = 84"; 84 ÷ 12" = 7' wide bed.

Go get your tape measure and measure 13'9" in. or 15'7" and see if you believe a natural descendent of Momma Eve (with good genes) would need a bed this long. Coupled with the belief in the scientific community that our ancestors were probably shorter than people are today, I would think we could come to the conclusion that Og was not natural human flesh in any sense of the word. This guy definitely had something wrong with his DNA!

When we consider Og and his kind, we understand the reason our Holy God had His agent, the Nation of Israel, utterly destroy the inhabitants of Canaan and surrounding lands. Since Israel would later produce the seed (through Judah) that would bear the Messiah, how fitting Israel (who gave us the Savior) would be God's agent (after the flood) to stop another attempt by Lucifer to contaminate the promised human Seed by destroying these perverted giants in the days of the patriarchs.

If you believe these giants in Genesis Chapter 6 were the result of the daughters of Cain marrying the sons of Seth, then, to be honest, you would need to figure out where the giants who lived in Canaan some four hundred fifty-five years[11] later originated and why this same type of union doesn't produce giants in 2009. Remember, God would not have destroyed the cities of Sodom and Gomorrah if there had been ten righteous people in this entire area. However, ungodly *lifestyle choices* had left only four (read Genesis Chapters 18–19).

I cannot help but wonder what the future holds for America with sexual perversion and genetic tampering on the rise!

NOTE: In the ancient Septuagint[12] (a translation of the Old Testament from Hebrew into Greek by seventy scholars from B.C. 280) Genesis 6:2 reads: **"The angels of God 'saw' the daughters of men."**

In 1 Corinthians 11:10 we read: "For this cause ought the woman to have power on *her* head **because of the angels**." This teaching is thought by some to be making reference to **evil angels** watching uncovered women. Would the Apostle Paul have had access to this ancient Septuagint translation of Genesis 6:2 as he wrote the Book of 1 Corinthians? I would certainly think so, him being taught by Gamaliel and having tremendous knowledge of the Old Testament. Also, I can remember in my younger days that it was a virtue for women *who were morally intact* to keep their bodies covered. I would not think all women knew about 1 Corinthians 11:10, but this moral tradition had been handed down from generation to generation. I would not be surprised if it was first taught by

---

11. Ussher, *Annals of the World*
12. Price, *Giants of Noah's Day*

those who knew about evil angels watching uncovered women and, thus, the instructions by God in A.D. 59[13] concerning the covering of the head.

In this day of marauding *immorality,* it would do the whole human family good to take notice of these and other Scriptures on this issue of angels "watching" our actions, especially women, since angels materialize in **male bodies.**

Brothers and sisters, we do not make the rules! We must come back to the understanding that Biblical authority produces purity. It is not determined by human thought or human actions! It can only be determined by Bible Words given to man by the Holy Spirit. First Corinthians 11:10 is still a part of our Bible Scripture. You don't find the will of God by taking a people poll on TV or the Internet! Read Psalm 12:6-7.

In *Antiquities of the Jews,* Book 1, chapter 3, and Book 5, chapter 2, the historian Josephus wrote:

> ... Many angels of God accompanied with women, and begat sons that proved unjust, and despisers of all that was good, on account of their own strength.... These men did what resembled the acts of those whom the Grecians called **giants.** ... There was till then left the race of **giants,** whom had bodies so large, and countenances **so entirely different from other men,** that they were **surprising to the sight,** and **terrible to the hearing.** The bones of these men are still shown to this very day, **unlike to any credible relations of other men.**

Wow! Josephus *actually* saw the bones of these giants in his day (about A.D. 80[14]). This causes me to wonder if they had museums in the Roman kingdom when Josephus was writing

---

13. Ibid.
14. Ibid.

this history. Maybe so!

The **Ante-Nicene Fathers,**[15] in commenting on Genesis 6:2, wrote that the **angels "fell into pure love of virgins, and were subjugated by the flesh.** . . . Of these lovers of virgins therefore, were begotten those who were called **giants**" (Vol. 2, p. 190; Vol. 3, pp. 85, 273).

Justin Martyr,[16] who lived between A.D. 110 and 165, commented on the conditions before the flood as based on the text in the Septuagint: ". . . the **angels transgressed, and were captivated by love of women and begat children**" (Vol. 2, p. 190).

Methodius,[17] who lived between A.D. 260 and 312, said: "The devil was insolvent. . . .As also those angels who were enamored of fleshly charms, **and had illicit intercourse with the daughters of men**" (Vol. 4, p. 370).

I think we have shown (from history and Scripture) the impending judgment of God on these *hybrid Antediluvian* peoples was a direct result of Genesis 6:2—**the sons of God marrying the daughters of men.** The fact that there was, **at one time, giants** living on Earth has been proven Biblically and by archaeological discovery! As we have stated in our historical references, bones were still in evidence in Josephus' day about A.D. 80.

However, we need not go back to A.D. 80 to see evidence of giants on Planet Earth. My wife and I have visited the Paluxy River Valley near Glen Rose, Texas, and **saw large human footprints embedded in the center of dinosaur footprints.** These dinosaur and human footprints were embedded together in soft sedimentary limestone at the time they were made. This limestone would later harden to preserve this scientific

---

15. Ibid.
16. Ibid.
17. Ibid.

evidence (very large humans and dinosaurs together) for the world to see in the twenty-first century.

Dr. Carl Baugh, at the Creation Evidences Museum, has done extensive work in this area and has uncovered **eighteen- to twenty-two-inch human footprints which I have personally viewed** in the riverbed of the Paluxy River. One only needs to take a ruler and measure eighteen to twenty-two inches to know, "That is a **big foot!**" I have just measured my left foot and found it to be ten and a half inches long. This is about normal for a five foot, eleven inch man. We know those big feet in this riverbed did not belong to normal men like Adam, Shem, Ham, or Japheth, or their wives, for they were on the ark which Noah had built (at the instruction of his Holy God)!

When the fountains of the deep erupted and belched out this fire, steam, water, and liquid sediment from the depths of this earth, these eight people were lifted up in the ark and saved by water (see 1 Peter 3:20). However, this same water that saved Noah and his family destroyed the rest of the people (who did not believe Noah's preaching) with the whole face of the Earth. In this process of destruction, these *Antediluvian peoples* were running for their lives, along with dinosaurs, laying down these huge footprints in this Paluxy River Valley area south of Fort Worth, Texas. This evidence is available for any open-minded person who cares to find the truth. All any skeptics need to do is go take a look!

"Sorry Charlie" Darwin: My God never leaves Himself without a witness! Praise His name! Amen and Amen!

There are those who use this Old Testament example of eight souls saved by water to try to encourage a New Testament doctrine of baptismal regeneration. After water baptism, *the saved* are to rise *up* in their body and walk in newness of life with a good conscience, as Noah and his family were to rise *up* in the ark and later walk in a new world to replenish it. Just as Noah was obedient to his God and found grace, the born-again believer (in the ordinance of baptism) has been obedient to his God and found grace. However, we must remember: salvation is tied to the grace of God and the blood of Jesus Christ, not to the works of man and the water in the river! Israel baptized in water under the Law of Moses, but the Law could never bring in the covenant of grace as Jesus Christ did *by the shedding of His blood* on the cross at Calvary! HOLY IS HIS NAME!

My dear friend, if you haven't taken time to come into the Ark of safety provided by Jesus Christ, please ask God the Holy Spirit to show you the way to safety. Be willing to follow His leadership, for it is truly, ". . . by grace are ye saved through faith; and that not of yourselves: it is the gift of God: Not of works, lest any man should boast" (Ephesians 2:8-9).

Note: God called Noah to preach. Noah preached while he built a boat. The world did not believe Noah's preaching. "It will never rain," they must have said. Noah preached and built anyway. After one hundred twenty *years,* God called Noah again. This time God said: "Come thou and all thy house **into** the ark; for thee have I seen righteous before me **in this generation."**

My friend, has God called you? Are you going **out** in the Rapture to meet Christ in the air or staying here on Earth?

In Genesis 8:15-16, we hear God call to Noah on the mountains of Ararat for the third time. We read: "And God spake unto Noah, saying, **Go forth** of the ark, thou, and thy wife, and thy sons, and thy sons' wives with thee."

They went forth into a new world. We will now *move forward* with Noah and his descendants to Chapter Four of this manuscript, where they *move* from **Ararat to Goshen** on their *journey* to go **Beyond the Revelation** and, eventually, get back to **The Last Eden.**

Chapter Four

From Ararat to Goshen

Just as many of us do in life today, all the children of Adam have made many *moves* in the six thousand-year history of mankind.

Before we look at Noah and the next *big move* he and his descendants will make into this third Dispensation where **Human Government** is designed to preserve this promised Seed, let me share my last big move prior to becoming an adult. I have already mentioned some of the *moves* my family made in my early life, but it seemed none were as devastating as this one.

I really believe that as we grow into young adulthood, we view things in a more personal way than we do when we are younger and more focused on our parents for leadership in a more intimate way.

And so, as I grew into my teens in the backwoods of Middle Tennessee, I started to hunt and trap. After hunting for skunk and opossum with my two first cousins, I soon discovered the fur market was very good. These cousins had a hunting dog named Ol' Blue, which was Australian shepherd and chow mix. This was, without a doubt, the most intelligent hunting dog that ever went into the woods on Lox Creek. It was not uncommon for us to harvest six skunks in one night's effort and be back to the house by ten p.m. Six skunks times three dollars equals eighteen dollars, minus shipping to Sears Roebuck = *almost* half a week's hard work at the shirt factory.

However, this was in the days before animal worship invaded America and the world.

At age fourteen, as soon as the season opened, I strung out my first trap-line. If I remember correctly, this was October 1957. Well, I was having the time of my life in this new adventure on my Aunt Callie's hillside farm. My new twenty-six-inch Western Flyer bicycle was the work-horse of my operation as I traveled up and down the road that ran by the creek. But, I also walked over the hills morning and evening to check and reset my steel traps and dead-falls.

Then (with my financial future looking bright) one night, to my total disbelief, I heard my Dad talking to my Mom about a house and four acres of land for sale, near the small town where I now reside. As I remember, it did not take but a few days for the deal to be struck. The announcement was made. We were *moving* from the area that I had lived all of my life to this house with just four acres of land. Well, my heart was crushed! It seemed to me as if we were *moving* to the backside of nowhere, when in reality we were only *moving* a few miles from where we lived!

As I remember, pulling out those traps seemed like the end of the world to me as a fourteen-year-old boy. You might be asking yourself about now, why all the sadness? Well, I had discovered from hunting with my cousins that if you work hard and do things right, people will pay you for your efforts! So, I pouted, wept, and moaned until the *move* was completed.

Soon, as people usually do, I began to adapt to my new environment and venture out. I soon discovered we had moved close to a fairly large river and a spring-fed creek, which was about half a mile behind our land, flowing through bottom-land fields that were being planted in corn. This was good news to a young farm boy who just wanted to get on with making some spending money. Through a very understanding Dad contacting landowners, plus a lot of early morning (before school) **hard walking and working,** I managed to bring in more pelts (muskrat, raccoon, mink, and opossum) than I could have caught from the hills and the creek running through my Aunt Callie's hillside farm.

As I remember, #1 red muskrats were bringing three dollars and fifty cents in 1957-58. This was big bucks in those day, when a dollar looked as big as a watermelon. In those days, the normal wage for part-time work was forty to fifty cents per hour. Large, good quality raccoons (properly skinned and stretched square) would bring eight to twelve dollars. Two large, quality raccoons would bring in more than a week's hard part-time labor for a fourteen-year-old hillbilly farm boy that had *moved* close to town!

When I say hard labor, I'm talking about one of my summer jobs which was mixing mortar with a mortar hoe and shovel, as well as carrying this mortar, plus concrete blocks, to place them on scaffolds for two experienced masons who knew their stuff! This particular summer, we built a fairly large Baptist church sanctuary in the middle of an open field where the only shade we had was the shade we built! **That's one hot job I will never forget!** As it turned out, this Baptist church sanctuary was located just up the road from where a beautiful young farm girl lived, who I would later ask to be my wife! Last year, I had the privilege of preaching the gospel at this sanctuary.

In my freshman and sophomore years of high school, I managed to start a decent bank account. I began to develop responsibilities and training proving very valuable in future life. I then took a job at a drive-in restaurant. I also continued to work part-time on a construction job installing septic systems with another one of my cousins. Between working part-time and dating my future wife full-time, the trap-line and bicycle riding just seemed to give way to the need for something with four wheels instead of two wheels! A 1957 black Chevy Belair was the first car I ever owned!

However, it seems everyone forgot to tell me, "Son, when you buy a car, you never get through paying because by the time you get one paid off, it is time to buy another!" For sure, if gasoline had been as high as it is these days, instead of twenty to thirty cents per gallon in those days, I might have been forced to keep my two-wheel bicycle for transportation that ran on my Momma's beans, meat, potatoes, and cornbread! This would have made the eight-mile-trip (one way) to my future wife's home very difficult, but then, probably not impossible!

I may cover more of my life's experiences later, but I will take time here to say that the beautiful fourteen-year-old gal that I was dating at this time has been my lovely wife for most of my life—and the rest of my life! We were married forty-seven years in June of this year. In our forty-seven years of married life, my wife and I have not agreed on everything, but one thing my wife and I have always agreed on is, when our God makes an eternal covenant, man should never try to put it asunder (see Matthew 19:6; Mark 10:9; and Genesis 6:15-21).

Now, back to Noah's life and our walk through God's Word, From Ararat to Goshen.

For Noah and his family members, the three hundred seventy-five days spent on the ark (see Genesis 7:11; 8:13-14) was, no doubt, an experience that no other group of peoples had experienced before or again up to this present time. I cannot begin to imagine the life-changing mental and physical experiences involved in this three hundred seventy-five-day *move* from a world of possibly millions of Antediluvian peoples to a new world of just eight people. If Mrs. Noah and her daughters-in-law had any new neighbors, they had to bear them through their own bodies and wait for them to grow up.

Let me insert here: This is the *unique move* of their time because Noah and his family members (after being freshly delivered from God's wrath "by water") never returned to the homes they left. This family is also a **unique family** because they survived universal judgment "by water" and arrived in a new world safe, sound, and blessed by God in the process.

In like manner, the saved family of God is some day going to make the **unique move** of their time because after the Rapture they will never return to the homes they left. They, too, will be a **unique family**, because the family of God will survive universal judgment by God's wrath on this planet to eventually arrive in the Millennial Kingdom, safe, sound, and blessed by God in the process.

Then, after the Millennium, will come the burning of this present Earth and the final judgment of God upon all sin (read Revelation 20:9-15). This **unique family** of God will make their final **unique move** to the New Heaven, New Earth, and holy New Jerusalem, safe, sound, and blessed by God in the process. They will never return to the old Heaven, old Earth and old Jerusalem, which was destroyed by consuming fire, because they are, finally, in **The Last Eden!** (Read Revelation 20:11; 21:1; 2 Peter 3:4-13).

Now, before I get too excited, let's get back to our walk with Noah:

As we see Noah and his family making their next *move,* having left the ark on the mountains of Ararat and beginning a new life on an Earth which had been judged by water, we hear the Lord say in Genesis 9:3-9:

Every moving thing **that liveth shall be meat for you;**

even **as** the green herb have I given you **all things.** But flesh with the life thereof, which is the blood thereof, shall ye not eat. And surely your blood of your lives will I require; at the hand of every beast will I require it, and at the hand of man; at the hand of every man's brother will I require the life of man. **Whoso sheddeth man's blood, by man shall his blood be shed: for in the image of God made he man.** And you, be ye fruitful, and multiply; bring forth abundantly in the earth, and multiply therein. And God spake unto Noah, and to his sons with him, saying, **And I, behold, I establish my covenant** with you, and with your seed after you [emphasis mine].

As God is making all these drastic changes after the flood, I wanted to personally thank Him for Genesis 9: 3 ("Every moving thing that liveth shall be meat for you"). As a Tennessee hillbilly Gentile who killed and cured his own hog meat for years, I cannot imagine a world without country ham and biscuits. (No offense to God's people who still believe they cannot eat pork). Please, read Romans Chapter 14.

Also, as we look at Genesis 9:9, it is obvious our God would not establish His covenant with just any seed because Scripture relates to us that God will incarnate Himself in Jesus Christ from the good seed (genes) of Noah through Mary in the future. (Read Isaiah 7:14 and Matthew 1:18-25).

As we go through this maze of historical happenings, we will see God is looking for a **man** and for a **people** whom He might use to bring His salvation to a future lost and ruined Jew and Gentile world.

I, personally, believe that what many people do not understand today is that this Seed of God (Jesus Christ) brought **complete Spiritual deliverance** at His first coming for whosoever will. I believe the Scriptures teach He will bring **com-**

plete physical deliverance as He raptures His espoused bride (the church), and seven years later He returns to Planet Earth by *moving* **Beyond the Revelation!** We will deal with this subject more thoroughly in later Chapters.

Neither time nor pen could express the love of this omnipotent, omnipresent, and omniscient God of love as He works His wondrous ways in the life of those who would love and obey Him! He truly is worthy to be praised for showing His patience to His Adamic creation and all Adam's sinful ways!

We must fast-forward at this time, coming to the next dispensation. We see a man born (eight generations forward from Shem) whose name was Terah. Terah was the father of a man whom God would later call to go into the land of Canaan! This man was **Abram!**

In Abram, we see the fourth Dispensation—**promise**—or the **Abrahamic Covenant** given to man. What exactly is this promise our God is making toward man? What does our wonderful God have on His mind as He selects Abram, calling he and his family to *move* into a land he has never seen which God alone can show him? Remember, God has *moved* Noah and his family to a new land. Now He is *moving* Abram and his family to a new land. I think we should ask ourselves: **What is God's purpose in all the *moving*?**

Is God still remembering Genesis 3:15 as He calls this son of Shem to go into this land of Canaan? Is there a **secret mission in Canaan** that our God has for Abram and his seed in the distant future? Let's look and see!

We read about Abram's big *move* into this new land in Genesis 12:1-7:

> Now the Lord had said unto Abram, Get thee out of thy country, and from thy kindred, and from thy father's house, unto a land that I will shew thee: And I will make of thee a

great nation, and I will bless thee, and make thy name great; and thou shalt be a blessing: And I will bless them that bless thee, and curse him that curseth thee: and in thee shall all families of the earth be blessed. So Abram departed, as the Lord had spoken unto him; and Lot went with him: and Abram was seventy and five years old when he departed out of Haran. And Abram took Sarai his wife, and Lot his brother's son, and all their substance that they had gathered, and the souls that they had gotten in Haran; and they went forth to go into the land of Canaan; and into the land of Canaan they came. And Abram passed through the land unto the place of Sichem, unto the plain of Moreh. **And the Canaanite was then in the land.** And the Lord appeared unto Abram, and said, Unto thy seed will I give this land: and there builded he an altar unto the Lord, who appeared unto him [emphasis mine].

As we notice the statement in Genesis 12:6, **"And the Canaanite was then in the land,"** I would like to take a moment expanding on this Verse if I can.

Who is the Canaanite? Why does God take the space to note in Scripture that he is in this land of promise that God is giving unto Abram and his seed?

To discover whom the Canaanite is and where the Canaanite originated, we will need to go back to Genesis 10. In Genesis 10:6,15–20 we read:

And the sons of **Ham;** Cush, and Mizraim, and Phut, and **Canaan** . . . And Canaan begat Sidon his firstborn, and Heth, And the Jebusite, and the Amorite, and the Girgasite, And the Hivite, and the Arkite, and the Sinite, And the Arvadite, and the Zemarite, and the Hamathite: and afterward were the families of the **Canaanites** spread abroad. And the border of the **Canaanites** was from Sidon, as thou comest to Gerar, unto Gaza; as thou goest, unto **Sodom, and Gomorrah,** and Admah, and Zeboim, even unto Lasha. These *are* the **sons of Ham,** after their families, after their tongues, in their countries, *and* in their nations [emphasis mine].

These Canaanites were some of the most perverse peoples we will find in all Scripture. What could have caused such perverseness in Adam's descendants, who no doubt had heard of the worldwide flood in the days of their forefathers? It had only been four hundred fifty-one years[18] since their father Ham walked off the ark onto the mountains of Ararat.

Some have suggested Ham was sexually perverse because of what happened in Genesis 9:20-27. In these seven Verses, Noah plants a vineyard, gets drunk from the wine he drank, and uncovers himself in his tent. Ham comes into the tent and sees his father's nakedness. Ham then told his two brothers which were on the outside of the tent. The two brothers took a garment and walked into the tent backward and covered their father. When Noah awoke from his wine, **he knew what his younger son had done unto him.** Noah then **places a curse on Ham's descendants, through Canaan; he also curses Ham's descendants to be the servants of both Shem and Japheth.**

Now, the mystery is: **What did Ham do?** Did Ham willfully plunge into sin and debauchery after the flood? Did he just look at Noah, or did he molest his father while he slept? The Bible does not say what Ham did, only that his descendants were cursed. Well, his descendants who populated Sodom and Gomorrah through his son, Canaan, *certainly willfully plunged into a perverse lifestyle of the baser sort* because the Scriptures

---

18. Ussher, *Annals of the World*

tell us in Genesis 13:13: "But the men of Sodom were wicked and sinners before the LORD exceedingly." If Ham did not *willfully* plunge into debauchery, then we would need to explain what he did to Noah causing a Holy God (through Noah) to curse Ham's son (Canaan) and his descendants. However, we as humans must remember that God knows the future and we do not. I do well to perceive the present!

Dr. N. W. Hutchings brings to light some very important information on page 37 of his book *The Whole Realm of Rebellion: Studies in Jude*. He writes:

> **The Canaanites were the most sexually debauched people on the face of the earth. Archaeological excavations have revealed that even their babies had venereal diseases. We must consider this awful condition as one reason why God commanded Israel to slay every Canaanite in the land, even the children.**

Also, in Genesis 19:1-5 God sent two angels (materialized in human male bodies) to destroy these wicked Canaanite cities of Sodom and Gomorrah. In these Verses, we hear these wicked men ask Lot (who had taken these two embodied angels into his home for the night): "Where are **the men** which came in to thee this night? Bring them out unto us that we may **know** [have sexual commerce with[19]] them."

In the middle of the night, in a mob environment, breaking down Lot's door is not the correct place or the time to get better acquainted with the latest guests to arrive in town.

If we compare the Hebrew word (*yaw-dah*) translated "know" in Genesis 19:5, with the Hebrew word (*yaw-dah*) translated "knew" in Genesis 4:1,25[20] where Adam impreg-

---

19. Webster, *American Dictionary of the English Language*
20. Strong, *Exhaustive Concordance*

nates Eve with children, we can see, contextually "we may *know* them" has to do with sexual commerce since both words are *yaw-dah* in the Hebrew dictionary.

We must realize that the cities of Sodom and Gomorrah were totally destroyed without mercy, just as the Earth had been in Noah's day. Only those that were (literally) brought out by the angels (materialized in human bodies) survived the judgment of these two cities of the plains. If we are honest with the Scriptures we should ask: *What happened?*

Abraham had pleaded with God to spare the cities if just ten righteous people could be found. All had chosen to abandon the way of righteousness, except four. One of those four, being Lot's wife, looked back and lost her life because of disobedience.

NOTE: Only eight people were delivered in the days of the flood and just four people were delivered out of Sodom and Gomorrah. I think we should look again and see if perversion has any bearing on these wholesale destructions brought about by God's supernatural judgment! When our God (who is love) cannot find any reason to have mercy on His prized creation, you can be sure something terrible has happened! It seems to me when people choose to become sexually perverse (in present or past societies) things definitely are bad. Add genetic perversion and you have a recipe for destruction from the Almighty! With both sexual and genetic tampering prevalent in today's society, what should we expect from our Creator in the near future? It seems that humanity under Lucifer's charm is more than willing to defy the most basic rules of human life set forth by Jesus Christ the Creator and is charting a collision course that can only lead to the same fiery confrontation as did Sodom, Gomorrah, and the pre-flood world!

And now, back to Genesis Chapter 12.

As we *move* farther into Genesis Chapter 12, we see Abram

forsaking this land of promise to go into Egypt in a time of grievous famine. Because of his fear of the Egyptians, he asked Sarai this favor: "Say, I pray thee, thou art my sister [she was his sister; see Genesis 20:12]: that it may be well with me for thy sake; **and my soul shall live because of thee.**"

Wow!!! What a prophecy.

This she does! Because of her beauty, Pharaoh takes her into his palace for an extended period of time. Pharaoh then showers Abram with many gifts. Abram **becomes very wealthy**. However, God plagues Pharaoh with great plagues because Sarai, Abram's wife, is living in his house. Upon discovery that she is Abram's wife, Pharaoh then commands his servants to send Abram and his wife out of the land of Egypt **with all Abram's possessions.**

We will now read Genesis 13:1-4:

> And Abram went up out of Egypt, he, and his wife, and all that he had, and Lot with him, into the south. And **Abram was very rich in cattle, in silver, and in gold.** And he went on his journeys from the south even to Bethel, unto the place where his tent had been at the beginning, between Bethel and Hai; Unto the place of the altar, which he had made there at the first: and there **Abram called on the name of the LORD** [emphasis mine].

We should note here: Abram became very rich while he was in Egypt. **Wealth** is something we will deal with more thoroughly in our next Chapter. However, I will say that what God did with Abram while he was in Egypt is a type of what God will do on a much more grand scale through Joseph in the future! But, we must not get into Chapter Five, just yet.

As we *travel* farther into Genesis 13, we see Lot and Abram separating because of the need for more herd space. Lot went to the plains toward Sodom and Gomorrah (as we have already discussed), and Abram remained in the land of Canaan.

After the separation, we hear God say to Abram in Genesis 13:14-15,18:

> And the LORD said unto Abram, after that Lot was separated from him, Lift up now thine eyes, and look from the place where thou art northward, and southward, and eastward, and westward: **For all the land which thou seest, to thee will I give it, and to thy seed for ever.** . . . Then Abram removed *his* tent, and came and dwelt in the plain of Mamre, which *is* in Hebron, and **built there an altar unto the LORD** [emphasis mine].

Some folks who claim to be Christians, don't know how long *forever* is. I pray anyone who would read this manuscript is not one of those people.

We should note here that this promise is being made by the only God of the universe in 1918 B.C.,[21] before the birth of the promised Seed which Abram and Sarai would bear in their old age.

As we *move* into Genesis 15, we hear God assuring Abram in Verse 4 that the promised Seed will come out of his own bowels. Verse 6 lets us know that Abram believed God and God counted it unto Abram for righteousness. After he questions God about how he would know he would inherit this land of Israel forever, in Verse 8 the Lord does a very unique thing. In Verses 9-17, He has Abram divide the offering parts of the animals, as was custom to do when a covenant was sealed between **two** individuals in those days.

Then, in a one-time event, God put Abram to sleep. God then walked between the bloody animal and fowl parts, sealing this covenant **by Himself,** thus making this covenant **to-**

---

21. Ussher, *Annals of the World*

tally unconditional on the part of Abraham or anyone who would follow!

Let's read just how God did it in Genesis 15:9-21:

And he said unto him, Take me an heifer of three years old, and a she goat of three years old, and a ram of three years old, and a turtledove, and a young pigeon. And he took unto him all these, and divided them in the midst, and laid each piece one against another: but the birds divided he not. And when the fowls came down upon the carcases, Abram drove them away. And when the sun was going down, **a deep sleep fell upon Abram; and, lo, an horror of great darkness fell upon him.** And he said unto Abram, Know of a surety that thy seed shall be a stranger in a land *that is* not theirs, and shall serve them; and they shall afflict them **four hundred years;** And also that nation, whom they shall serve, will I judge: **and afterward shall they come out with great substance** [more on this in Chapter Five]. And thou shalt go to thy fathers in peace; thou shalt be buried in a good old age. But in **the fourth generation** they shall come hither again: **for the iniquity of the Amorites** *is* **not yet full** [Amorites: descendants of Canaan, Gen. 10:15-16]. And it came to pass, that, when the sun went down, and it was dark, behold a smoking furnace, and a burning lamp that passed between those pieces. **In the same day the LORD made a covenant with Abram, saying, Unto thy seed have I given this land, from the river of Egypt unto the great river, the river Euphrates: The Kenites, and the Kenizzites, and the Kadmonites, And the Hittites, and the Perizzites, and the Rephaims, And the Amorites, and the Canaanites, and the Girgashites, and the Jebusites** [emphasis and commentary mine].

Wow! That's a lot of land! I wonder if the present-day seed of Abraham is in line for a **border enlargement** in the not too distant future.

As we come into Genesis Chapter 16, we once again discover one of the more **subtle attempts of Lucifer to destroy this promised Seed of God** that would bring salvation to the whole world!

Sarai, Abram's wife, becomes very impatient with God because she was barren. In her desperation, she decides to take matters into her own hands and produce this promised Seed for God (whether He wants it or not).

If our God had permitted this Egyptian bond-slave to fulfill Sarai's plan in the birth of Ishmael, the whole human family would have come under the **curse of Ham** and Jesus Christ would not have been born of the seed of Shem, through Isaac, and eventually through David as God had promised.

The Scriptures remind us of this **curse of Ham through his son Canaan** in Genesis 9:25. We read, **"And he said, Cursed be Canaan; a servant of servants shall he be unto his brethren."**

In Genesis 16:12, we read the prophecy the angel gives to this **servant** of Sarai about Ishmael and what he would become. **"And he will be a wild man; his hand will be against every man, and every man's hand against him; and he shall dwell in the presence of all his brethren."**

I think we should note that it was not Hagar's doing that Ishmael would be born from Abram. It was an impatient Sarai and a perfectly willing Abram. It almost sounds as if Abram is thinking, *Sounds like the perfect will of God to me that Sarai would give me her bond-servant to be my young wife* (read Galatians 4:30).

Just as the two impatient daughters of Lot will, in the future, get him drunk and have intercourse to produce Moab and Ammon through incest by their father (see Genesis 19:30-38),

Hagar is with child and will bear Ishmael. These three women would have done well if they could have realized that obedience truly is better than sacrifice.

We will note here: Samuel the prophet speaks to King Saul on this matter of obedience as God is about to depose him from the kingship of Israel. We read 1 Samuel 15:22–23: "And Samuel said, Hath the LORD as great delight in burnt-offerings and sacrifices, as in obeying the voice of the LORD? Behold, **to obey is better than sacrifice, and to hearken than the fat of rams.** For rebellion is as the sin of witchcraft, and stubbornness is as iniquity and idolatry. **Because thou hast rejected the word of the LORD, He hath also rejected thee from being king.**"

Just as King Saul truly believed he could do a better job of running God's business than God could, these three women (Sarai and Lot's two daughters), with the best of intentions, **have brought about an opportunity for the devil to attempt to spoil the genetic plan of a Redeemer for all mankind, Jesus Christ!**

Also, if we were to look at the enemies of Israel from Abraham down to this present day, I think we would conclude the descendants of Ishmael, Ammon, and Moab (who came out of the loins of Lot and Abram in their times of weakness) have been some of the most bitter enemies of all the peoples surrounding this chosen nation. If we were to throw Esau and a few other haters of God's covenant people into the mix, we would come up with fifty to seventy million modern-day descendents who have despised and devised Israel's complete destruction since May 14, 1948. Add in Satan's agent, the United Nations, as well as America's "land for peace" onslaught, and it seems to me you have a recipe for the war and supernatural destruction of nations recorded in Ezekiel Chapters 38–39. Then, mix in a Satan incarnate called the Antichrist who will fill the vacuum created by the Ezekiel Chapters 38–39 war, and the whole world will soon be poised for Armageddon! Then, ride from the third Heaven on your white horse back to Planet Earth with the King of all Kings and the Lord of all Lords (Revelation 19:11–16) and you will have just at that moment *moved* **Beyond the Revelation!**

Glory to God!!!

Now, before I get too carried away and spoil this manuscript, let's get back to the conclusion of our *trip*—FROM ARARAT TO GOSHEN.

As we journey into Genesis Chapter 17, we see Abram and Sarai receiving a name change. We read:

> And when Abram was **ninety years old and nine,** the LORD appeared to Abram, and said unto him, I am the Almighty God; walk before me, and be thou perfect.... As for me, behold, my covenant is with thee, and thou shall be a father of many nations. Neither shall thy name any more be called Abram, **but thy name shall be Abraham;** for a father of many nations have I made thee. And I will establish **my covenant** between me and thee, and thy seed after thee in their generations **for an everlasting covenant,** to be a God unto thee, and to thy seed after thee. **And I will give unto thee, and to thy seed after thee, the land wherein thou art a stranger,** *all* **the land of Cannan, for an everlasting possession; and I will be their God.** ... And ye shall circumcise the flesh of your foreskin; and it [circumcision] shall be a token of **the covenant betwixt me and you.** ... And God said unto Abraham, As for Sarai thy wife thou shall not call her name Sarai, **but Sarah [princess] shall her name be.** And I will bless her and give thee a son also of her: yea, I will bless her, and **she shall be a mother of nations; kings of people shall be of her.** Then Abraham fell upon his face,

and laughed, and said in his heart, Shall a child be born unto him that is **an hundred years old**? and shall Sarah, that is **ninety years old**, bear? And Abraham said unto God, O that Ishmael might live before thee! And God said, Sarah thy wife shall bear thee a son indeed; and thou shalt call his name **Isaac**; and I will establish my covenant with him for an everlasting covenant, and with his seed after him. . . . But my covenant will I establish **with Isaac**, which Sarah shall bear unto thee **at this set time in the next year.** . . . And Abraham was ninety years old and nine, when he was circumcised in the flesh of his foreskin.
—Genesis 17:1,4–5,7–8,11,15–19,21,24
[emphasis and commentary mine]

Wow! **What a miracle in the working.** Here we have a man ninety-nine years old and a woman eighty-nine years old. They are about to start a family in just twelve months. You need not be a rocket scientist to figure out that people in this age bracket don't have kids.

But God made a promise to Abraham. He plans to keep it to the fullest, even if it means stepping on Satan and all his illegitimate cronies he has produced in his perverted attempts on the promised Seed!

Continuing our *journey* into Genesis 21, we see this miracle baby, **Isaac, born to Abraham at age one hundred** (just as God had promised) and being circumcised the eighth day. Later we also see Ishmael mocking Isaac and Sarah, becoming very angry with him and his mother.

After some instructions from God, we see Hagar taking Ishmael and leaving the household of Abraham, traveling into the wilderness of Beer-sheba. The angel of God then speaks to Hagar, telling her God will make a great nation of her son. Then, we watch Ishmael grow up in the wilderness and **marry**

an Egyptian.

Arriving in Genesis Chapter 22, we see **Isaac about to be offered by Abraham** on Mount Moriah. This is, without any doubt, one of the most beautiful typologies in all of the Old Testament. We join Isaac in his humble conversation to his father in Verses 7–8. We read: "And Isaac spake unto Abraham his father, and said, My father: and he said, Here am I, my son. And he said; behold the fire and the wood: but where is the lamb for a burnt offering? And Abraham said, My son, **God will provide *himself* a lamb** for a burnt offering: so they went both of them **together**."

I will take time at this point in our *journey* to praise my Holy God that we do not see the son of an Egyptian bond-slave sitting on this donkey as Abraham and his son, Isaac, ride off **together** toward Mount Moriah. If a bond-slave's son had been on the donkey with Abraham, the salvation of the whole human family would have been destroyed. We must now pick up the pace, *moving* toward the Land of Goshen.

In Genesis Chapter 23, Sarah dies at the age of one hundred twenty-seven years and is buried in the cave of the Machpelah.

In Genesis Chapter 24, Abraham seeks out a bride, Rebekah, for Isaac among his father's people in Mesopotamia in the city of Nahor.

In Genesis Chapter 25, Abraham marries another wife named Keturah who bore this hundred-year-old-plus patriarch five sons. Talk about strong genes! God surely blessed this man Abraham! However, as life takes its toll on all mankind, so it did on this man of God, for in Verse 8 Abram dies at the good old age of one hundred seventy-five years.

In this same Chapter, Ishmael dies fifty-seven years later,[22]

---

22. Ibid.

at the age of one hundred fifty-seven years, and after having twelve sons.

Jacob and Esau are born to Rebekah. Afterward, we hear God promise her that the elder shall serve the younger. This is accomplished, in part, by Esau selling Jacob his birthright because he cared nothing about this **promised Seed** who would come from Isaac's loins. Thus, Esau despised his birthright (Genesis 25:34b).

In Genesis Chapter 26, we see Isaac's lapse in faith as he dwells at Gerar in Egypt because of a famine in his land. Once again, we see (as we did with Abram in Egypt) Isaac telling the men of Gerar that his wife, Rebekah, is his sister. He feared the Egyptians would kill him and take his wife because she was fair to look upon. After Isaac had been in Egypt for a long time, Abimelech saw Isaac sporting with Rebekah and confronted him. As it had been with Abraham, this was the beginning of Isaac becoming very wealthy and being driven back home to Beer-sheba.

As we come to Genesis Chapter 27, we sometimes hear it said Jacob stole the blessing from Esau. But, did Jacob steal the blessing or did Esau lose it to Jacob willingly because of the events recorded in the last part of Chapter 25?

We must take note: The birthright was of no value to Esau because he was a man destitute of faith in God. Thus, as already noted, the birthright was despised. However, we must not lose sight of the Bible facts on this matter of Jacob and Esau, as we hear the LORD answering Rebekah's inquiry in Genesis 25:23. We read: "**And the LORD said** unto her, **two nations** are in thy womb, and **two manner of people** shall be separated from thy bowels; and the one people shall be stronger than the other people; **and the elder shall serve the younger.**"

What was God trying to tell this mother of twins when they would come from her womb as Jacob was holding to Esau's heel? Was it God's plan all along for Jacob (who honored the birthright and the promised blessing) to receive both the birthright and the blessing from Isaac? Was Rebekah wiser than her husband, Isaac, as she remembered the Words of God ("the elder shall serve the younger")? Is this why she helped orchestrate the blessing from Isaac to Jacob?

Let's look at Romans 9:6-13 and see if the New Testament will shed light in this matter. We read:

> Not as though the word of God hath taken none effect. For they are not all Israel, which are of Israel: Neither, because they are the seed of Abraham, are they all children: but, **in Isaac shall thy seed be called.** That is, They which are the children of the flesh, these are not the children of God: **but the children of the promise are counted for the seed.** For this is the word of promise, at this time will I come and Sarah shall have a son. And not only this; but when Rebekah also had conceived by one, even by our father Isaac; (For the children being not yet born, neither having done any good or evil, that the purpose of God according to election might stand, **not of works, but of Him that calleth:**) It was said unto her, the elder shall serve the younger. As it is written, Jacob have I loved, but Esau have I hated [emphasis and commentary mine].

What is our God trying to say in these Verses? Simply, that the things of God come to men and women of faith (see Romans 9:32).

I think we should all stand up and give Rebekah a hand of applause!

Hebrews 12:16-17 gives us the fate of this God-rejecting Esau. We read: "Lest there be any **fornicator, or profane person, as Esau,** who for one morsel of meat sold his birthright. For ye know how that afterward, **when he would have inher-**

ited the blessing, he was rejected: for he found no place of repentance, though he sought it, carefully, with tears."

How sad that Esau came so close, yet missed the eternal blessings of God.

As we leave Genesis Chapter 27, we hear Esau planning the murder of his brother, Jacob, in verse 41. Once again, this God-hater shows his true nature. (Read the little Book of Obadiah on future events, especially Verse 10.)

Note: Because of the Scriptures I've listed, I take issue with the words "the stolen blessing" in my Bible commentary. In fact, quite the contrary is true. If Esau had been placed in line to produce this promised seed through which Jesus Christ would be born; this world would be in a spiritual mess because Satan would ultimately have won the battle. (Remember Genesis 3:15.) *Such commentaries are nothing short of "mild" Jew bashing!*

Let's admit it. *God-haters don't produce seed from which would be born the Messiah and Savior of the human family! Amen!*

In Chapter 28 of our journey, we find Jacob being sent to Padan-aram in order to escape Esau's death threat, taking a wife from Laban, Rebekah's brother. **Thus, another attempt by Esau to destroy this promised Seed is aborted!** During his trip to Padan-aram, Jacob has a dream and sees a ladder reaching from Earth to Heaven, with the angels of God ascending and descending on it. He then sees God standing above this ladder and hears God confirm the promised [land] covenant to him that God had already promised to Abraham and Isaac (Verse 3). God then promises Jacob in Verse 14b that "in thee and **in thy seed** shall all the families of the earth be blessed."

As we walk through Genesis Chapters 29-35, we see Jacob take not one but two wives because of the trickery of his uncle, Laban. We then see eleven sons born to Jacob and his two wives through some very unusual circumstances, to say the least. Jacob then uses his wisdom to foil Laban's trickery and make himself rich from Laban's cattle, sheep, and goats by manipulating the birth process.

Moving farther on our journey toward Goshen, God calls Jacob to come back to Bethel, the land of his kindred. After this, Jacob is alone at the brook Jabbok. Here, he wrestles with a man until the breaking of day. Jacob refuses to let this man go until he blesses him. As it turns out, this man is none other than the pre-incarnate Christ. It is here God changes Jacob's name to Israel.

In Genesis 32:30, we read: "And Jacob called the name of the place Peniel: **For I have seen *God* face to face, and my life is preserved**" [emphasis mine].

Jacob then meets Esau and they are reunited. **Esau then returns to Seir, his home,** and Jacob stops in the land of Cannan at Shechem, spreading his tent. This proves to be a great mistake because Shechem, the son of Hamor, the prince of the land, defiles Dinah, Jacob's daughter by Leah.

Hamor, a Canaanite, again **attempts to (as in the past) infiltrate the promised seed** by persuading Jacob and his sons and daughters **to intermarry with the sons and daughters of Canaan.** Jacob's sons then trick Hamor and all the males of his city into being circumcised. While they were sore, Simeon and Levi took their swords into the city, slaying every male. **They took Dinah out of Shechem's house, once again foiling Satan's evil plan to infiltrate the promised seed and stop the birth of Messiah.**

They then spoiled the whole city and all the inhabitants. God again speaks to Jacob in Genesis Chapter 35 and commands him to return to Bethel, **where he is to receive a name change from Jacob to Israel.** Here at Bethel God reconfirms the covenant He had previously made with Abraham and Isaac,

Jacob's fathers. We read Genesis 35:12: "And **the land** which I gave Abraham and Isaac, to thee will I give it, and to thy seed after thee will I give the land."

Jacob then resumes his journey toward Hebron, and as he is in Ephratah (Bethlehem) Rachel travailed in labor. We read Genesis 35:17-18: "And it came to pass, when she was in hard labor, that the midwife said unto her, Fear not; thou shalt have this son also. And it came to pass, as her soul was in departing, (for she died) she called his name Ben-oni: but his father called him Benjamin [**son number twelve**]."

We then see Jacob come into Hebron to his father, Isaac, who soon dies at the age of one hundred and eighty years.

In Genesis Chapter 36, we see the generations of Esau recorded. Here, the Scriptures make it very clear in Genesis 36:43b that Esau is the father of all the Edomites.

In Genesis Chapter 37 we conclude Chapter Four of this manuscript as we see Jacob and his beloved son, Joseph, who is now seventeen years old. But Joseph's brothers hated him because his father loved him more than all his other children. They also despised his coat of many colors, which Jacob had made for him. And it came to pass when Joseph was sent to Shechem, where his brothers were keeping their father's sheep, his brothers took off his coat of many colors and cast Joseph into a pit to die. They later decided to sell Joseph to a band of Ishmaelite merchants for **twenty pieces of silver**. The merchants brought Joseph into Egypt near the land of Goshen.

Realizing this has been a long and difficult *journey,* **from Ararat to Goshen**, I sincerely hope I have not wearied your patience.

We will, with God's help, find this Joseph again in Chapter Five of this manuscript. He will be very instrumental in our examination of **wealth** as we continue our *journey through Scripture* going **Beyond the Revelation** into **The Last Eden.**

Chapter Five

From Goshen to the Kingdom

As we continue our *journey* through Scripture taking us **Beyond the Revelation to The Last Eden**, have you ever wondered what will happen to all of the wealth God has permitted mankind to accumulate over the centuries? Some, no doubt, would answer this question with: *God will burn the wealth, with this planet, as soon as He Raptures His Church to Heaven!*

Well, I, for one, do not believe consuming fire is the correct answer to every question we are asked concerning **future things**. I think that sometimes people use this to evade searching out truth in the Words of God.

We should look into God's Word to get our answers and not speculate with human reasoning. Our ideas (if they are incorrect) will only lead to confusion and loss of rewards in the future Kingdom of God's Holy Son, Jesus Christ. *Being good stewards of the Word should be an integral part of every Christian portfolio.*

Those who are good stewards know from God's precious Holy Word that this sin-crazed world will not continue on this path of prosperity forever. From the look of things for the last few months, the pie in the sky has already fallen back to Earth and the international bankers have eaten their fill!

In Chapter Five, we will continue on our *journey* toward God's Last Eden and at the same time do an examination on the beginning of wealth; also, we will look at how God **has and will** use wealth for His glory as He *moves* His promised Seed closer toward Calvary to begin the head-bruising of Lucifer prophesied in Genesis 3:15.

I will not be looking so much at the well-to-do family that lives in Beverly Hills in their estate mansion, or the poor family in South Texas who suddenly finds they are gushing in light, sweet, crude oil. What we will look at is a much larger program of wealth being orchestrated by the Triune Godhead and written in our **Holy Christian Bible.**

Someone once said: *God has nothing to do in this matter of personal finance. This comes about by the personal decisions we make in life.* Well, if you believe that, just continue reading, my friend, because God's Word has a different explanation of the matter.

It would stagger everyone's imagination if we could know the massive amounts of gold, silver, other precious metals, and gems of all shapes and forms which individuals, governments, religious organizations, foundations, cults, etc. have amassed since the days of Joseph.

Do the Words of our Lord have anything to say concerning who has in the past and will in the future acquire all of this massive wealth as time winds down to the end of this dispensation?

As we move into Chapter Five, I will examine this question and attempt to answer it from the God's Word, to be sure our God has His hand in this matter, just as He does in all matters of this universe.

Also, as we examine this issue **in the Bible**, we will look at how this subject of **wealth** actually helps to bring us **Beyond the Revelation,** preparing us for the entrance into **The Last**

Eden! As we make this examination, we should remember God is in full control.

Since we read in the Scriptures, "The earth is the Lord's and the fullness thereof, the world, and they that dwell therein" (Psalm 24:1), you can know our God has something wonderful in mind concerning this wealth for His Saints. More on this, later!

I have noticed since I started to research this subject that if you try to discuss the Biblical issue of wealth with many of God's people, they look at you as if you have fallen out of a tree on your head or, even worse, they seem to think you are just plain crazy! Well, I assure you, I have neither fallen out of a tree on my head nor am I crazy (at least in my opinion).The pure Words of my Holy God will stand when this planet is dissolved by consuming fire. Amen.

Now, let's work our way back to Joseph at Goshen, and continue to examine wealth in God's Holy Scriptures and see just how God is using it to His glory and purpose.

As we live on Earth, there are many things that come and go year in and year out. They just pass us by, and we never stop and take time to think, *Why do these things exist? Why are some people wealthy, and others as poor as blue clay dirt? Why do some people work hard all of their lives and never accomplish very much wealth, while others work very little in life and accumulate a large fortune?*

Dr. B. R. Lakin once said, "Surely, God must have loved the poor people because He made so many of them."

This brings us to the question: How do people obtain wealth? Is it just by accident? Do they acquire it by birth? Well, it would help if their parents were multimillionaires; however, many times that is not the case. Does God have a hand in who becomes wealthy and who doesn't become wealthy? Let's see if we can find the answers to these questions by looking at what God has done in the past. This is always a good barometer for the prophetic future.

For many years, we have lived in a time of prosperity such as this world has never known. **We must understand that wealth never ceases to exist;** it only changes hands and, believe me, a lot has changed hands recently. AMEN!!! Does God have a plan for this wealth the nations are amassing? I think the Bible will verify that He does.

Many people think it is an act of good fortune if you become wealthy, or that fortune failed to smile on you if you stay poor.

We who have studied the Holy Scriptures concerning prophecy know better. There is only one God who rules and reigns over the kingdoms of men, and I know His name! In His **Triunity** (Father, Son, Holy Ghost), He is working in the affairs of men on a daily basis.

We could ask ourselves: *Where is the wealth of precious metals that have been gathered in the past centuries? Where is the gold that people around the world "cashed in" when prices went to over eight hundred dollars per ounce?* As gold is at the time of this writing moving at over eleven hundred dollars per ounce, will this cause an even greater meltdown of the vast amount of jewelry and other items that are made of gold and silver? Does the Denver Mint, Fort Knox, and other places still hold the vast gold reserves they once held when our money was on the gold and silver standard? Will "Pay to the Bearer on Demand" (once printed on every piece of paper money) always be a dream of the past? Why is God permitting a large amount of this wealth to accumulate into the Middle East through the sale of oil? Does God have a special plan for this wealth as we travel on this Earth toward the New Earth *(**The Last Eden**)?*

As I said earlier, I would like to look and see if we can answer these questions and others from His Holy Word and from other historical sources.

If we were to look in our Webster's Dictionary at the definition of wealth, we would find the following given: "Happiness; much money or property; great amounts of worldly possessions; riches."

The root word of "wealth" is *weal* which means: "A sound or prosperous state; well being: welfare." This gives us the basis for the definition of happiness, and why not? Surely if a person is in a sound or prosperous state, and has well being, they should be very happy, right?

Well, we know the human family has for almost six thousand years sought happiness in prosperity, and as it has been in the past, so it is today. In my personal experience, the only true happiness came when I was born again by the Holy Spirit, became saved and forgiven of my sins, and started a proper stewardship of my finances toward God and His work in His holy New Testament Church.

We have an abundance of prosperity religions in this world pumping out sermon after sermon on the subject of "gain is godliness" and are ignoring **"ye must be born again"** (see Addendum B). Preaching prosperity theology to obtain happiness is like beating a dead horse with a stick in hopes he will stand up for you to take a ride. The only way we, as Christians, can be happy with our money is through hard work and a proper stewardship taught by the Bible and led by the Holy Spirit.

However, a wonderful brother in Alabama told me that the way to be happy is to "walk your talk." His philosophy was: If you are not walking your talk, don't tell me how to walk. I do believe this blessed brother has a good point in his evaluation of "happiness."

I have watched in my few short years of living on Earth, and have noticed men and women as they start out in life.

They are full of vim and vigor as they start working, saving, buying, selling, moving in and out, always looking and searching for that one possession which will make them more secure and happy. Then, I watch as these same people grow older and their health begins to **fail**. The body begins to **slow**, wrinkles begin to **grow**, their energy begins to **go**, the grass gets much more difficult to **mow**, the truth about their humanity begins to **show**, then the realization begins to **flow**: Hey! Some day, I am going to die and leave this world and who is going to wind up with all these possessions I have worked and slaved for all my life while on Earth? Good question, I would think! Someone might say: *Well, they will probably leave it all to their children when they "kick off" to eternity.* That could and probably would be a good guess, but everyone's children are riding in the same boat their parents are. They also are going to either die or be Raptured off Planet Earth.

The truth of the matter is: Some day—I do not know when—Christ will return to the air to call His bride "up" to meet Him.

Then, every Christian—wealthy or broke as a convict—will leave all their earthly possessions behind on Earth. This causes me to wonder: *What will happen to all of the wealth that Christians (as well as others) have amassed on Earth after they leave?* One thing is for sure: the only part of their wealth they can take with them **is what they have given away for God's work to be accomplished on Earth**. We could speculate and say there will always be a next of kin, but that will not be the case in many instances. As we have already noted, personal wealth is only a drop in the bucket when you compare it to the wealth of governments, some apostate churches, many organizations, pension funds, endowments, corporations, cults, etc. As we ponder this thing of acquiring wealth, let's ask ourselves three questions.

1. **When** in history did this **acquisition of wealth** begin?
2. **Where** did this **idea of acquiring wealth** come from?
3. **What** will be the **end result of acquiring this wealth?**

Now, we will attempt to answer these questions (in order) from the God's Holy Word.

Answer to question # 1.

All this wealth acquisition began with Joseph (Israel's son of his old age).

For this account, we will need to go back to Genesis Chapter 37 (B.C. 1715)[23] and once again join Joseph as he is being sold into Egypt by his brothers.

As we ended Chapter Four, we saw Joseph hated and rejected by his brothers and in time he was cast into a pit to die by the same. Had it not been for Reuben and Judah, Joseph would have been killed because of jealousy. But, Joseph's God had a greater plan for Joseph. All of my life, I have heard it preached and taught that Joseph was sent ahead into Egypt as a forerunner and deliverer of Israel, his father, and his brethren. We can see this is a Biblical truth.

We read in Genesis 37:28,36: "Then there passed by Midianites merchantmen; and they drew and lifted up Joseph out of the pit, and sold Joseph to the Ishmeelites for **twenty pieces of silver:** and they brought Joseph into Egypt. . . . And the Midianites sold him into Egypt unto Potiphar, an officer of Pharaoh's, and captain of the guard."

It has been shown in numerous places that Joseph is, in type, what Jesus Christ would become in reality. **As we pass by on our *journey*, we will look at eight things that show this typology.**

1. They were both greatly loved of their father.

---

23. Ussher, *Annals of the World*

2. Both were hated by their brethren.
3. Both were sold for money: Joseph sold for twenty pieces of silver (Genesis 37:28); Jesus for thirty pieces of silver (Matthew 26:15).
4. Both the claims of Joseph and Jesus were rejected by their brethren.
5. Both had an attempt made on their life by their brethren.
6. As for intent, each of these men were killed by their brethren.
7. Both Joseph and Jesus Christ would gain a Gentile bride and become a blessing among the Gentiles.
8. Joseph in time reconciled his brethren to himself and promoted them. So it will someday be with Christ to His brethren (Israel) because He will also promote them nationally when He shall reign as King over the nations of this Earth (see Isaiah 41:8-16; Jeremiah 30:8-24; 31:1-12,27-28; Revelation 9:16).

As this is beautiful and fulfilling to note, I see still another far-reaching reason for Joseph being sent into Egypt which I will attempt to show.

In Genesis Chapter 39 we see the account of Joseph in Egypt as God is testing him with Potiphar's wife, who falsely accuses Joseph of sexual advances. Even though Joseph was completely innocent, he was cast into prison because of her lies. However, God was with Joseph and showed him great mercy and gave him favor in the sight of the keeper of the prison. God **gave Joseph** the power of interpretation to interpret dreams. **Please, keep these gifts of God in mind as we *move* farther into Chapter Five.**

In Genesis Chapter 41 we find that Pharaoh "dreamed a dream." As he stood by the river (in his dream), Pharaoh saw seven fat kine (cattle) and seven lean kine come up out of the river. Then, the seven lean kine "ate" the seven fat kine. So, Pharaoh awoke!

Answer to question #2 on page 98.

It is in this dream of Pharaoh that we see one of the most significant beginnings of wealth acquisition in all the history of the then-known world!

The chief butler reminds Pharaoh he remembers a Hebrew in the prison who has the ability to interpret his dream. Pharaoh immediately calls for Joseph. Joseph interprets Pharaoh's dream and tells of seven good years of plenty, and warns of seven bad years of famine wherein there will be drought in Egypt. It is then that Joseph does an amazing thing. Because of his wisdom **from God**, he suggests that Pharaoh take **one-fifth** of all the fruits of Egypt and **store** these fruits in special cities. This food will be in the land for the seven bad years of famine.

We read in Genesis 41:39-40: "And, Pharaoh said unto Joseph, Forasmuch as **God hath shewed thee** all of this, there is none so discrete and wise as thou art: Thou shalt be over my house, and **according unto thy word shall all my people be ruled: only in the throne will I be greater than thou.**"

In the following Verses, Joseph is given a **Gentile bride**. It is very interesting to note that this Gentile bride is given at a time when Joseph has been rejected by his brethren and sent to a distant land. This is a perfect type of Jesus being rejected by His brethren and going to a distant land to receive a **Gentile bride**, the New Testament church, which will be caught up in the air to Him at the Rapture. While Joseph was in this distant land, he preserved his father and family by selling them grain and, ultimately, bringing Israel and his family, totaling seventy people, to live in Egypt **at Goshen.**

Though this completes the journey from Ararat to Goshen, it does not complete our story on wealth acquisition by

Israel's God. Also, we must move **from Goshen to the Kingdom in this Chapter.**

It is evident there is a great truth overlooked in this story most of the time. I feel we must give careful notice to Genesis 47:13-17. We read:

> And there was no bread in all the land; for the famine was very sore, So that the land of Egypt and all the land of Cannan fainted by reason of the famine. And Joseph **gathered up all the money** that was found in the land of Egypt, and in the land of Canaan, for the corn which they bought: **and Joseph brought the money into Pharaoh's house.** And when money failed in the **land of Egypt**, and in the **land of Cannan**, all of the Egyptians came unto Joseph, and said, Give us bread: for why should we die in thy presence? **for the money faileth.** And Joseph said, Give your cattle; and I will give you for your cattle, if money fail. And they brought their cattle unto Joseph: and Joseph gave them bread in exchange for horses, and for the flocks, and for the cattle of the herds, and for the asses: and he fed them with bread for all their cattle for that year [emphasis mine].

As we continue to read Verses 18 through 26, we see Joseph not only acquired for Pharaoh **all the money, cattle, horses, flocks, and asses,** but he **acquired the peoples' land and bodies.** He (in reality) took total control of Egypt and Canaan for the Pharaoh. He then put the people in cities and made them sow and work Pharaoh's lands. The people in turn had to give Pharaoh **one-fifth** of the increase and keep **four-fifths** for themselves. It is easy to see almost two thousand years before Christ was born that when things got really bad, people were very willing to sell out to the government in order to live. Sounds a little like today, doesn't it?

We should note: The tax rates of this present government are higher for most people than those Joseph levied on these peoples. It is likely these rates in America will go much higher in the next four years. However, in this case it was for a special purpose which we will see later.

In Exodus Chapter 1, we find that Joseph has died. The Israelites have greatly multiplied in the land of Egypt. It is at this time that **a Pharaoh arose that knew not Joseph**. This Pharaoh turned Israel to slavery and the people cried for a deliverer. It was then that God heard their cries and raised up Moses out of the house of Levi to be a deliverer of his brethren.

What was our God's purpose for bringing Israel (Jacob) out of his home country of Canaan into Egypt for his descendants to live for over four hundred years? Why did God not prosper him in his own land, as He did in Egypt? Good questions.

I think, as we go farther, we will see how God is using all of these men and nations to accomplish his will. It has to do with keeping the "seed of promise" pure, and at the same time, the gathering of wealth for God's Holy purpose.

We will now *move forward to find out what God has in mind for Israel and all this wealth of Egypt.*

In Exodus Chapter 2, we see Moses (after being born of Levite parents and raised in Pharaoh's house by his daughter) identifying with his Israelite brothers because he saw an Egyptian smiting a Hebrew. After fleeing from Pharaoh, Moses finds himself living in the land of Midian in Reuel's tent. Reuel is referred to as Jethro, priest of Midian, in Exodus 3:1. Moses takes a Gentile bride (of Reuel's daughters) while in this distant land. But back in Egypt, things have become more intolerable for the children of Israel. We read in Exodus 2:23-25:

> And it came to pass in process of time, that the king of Egypt died: and the children of Israel sighed by reason of the

bondage, and they cried, and their cry came up unto God by reason of the bondage. And **God heard** their groaning, and **God remembered** His covenant with Abraham, with Isaac, and with Jacob. And **God looked** upon the children of Israel, and **God had respect** unto them [emphasis mine].

Moses is then commissioned of God to return to Egypt, where he is seen in contest with Pharaoh to let God's people, Israel, go forth from the land. And, I might add, also to take **all of the gold, silver, precious stones, clothing of all sorts, and wealth in general with them.**

It is amazing in Scripture how these two men—**Joseph and Moses**—were used of God.

Joseph was used to gather Israel, his kindred, and all of the wealth in the region *into* Pharaoh's kingdom.

Moses was used to remove a much greater and mightier Israel, with all of this wealth of Egypt *out* of Pharaoh's kingdom. Wow, what a God!

Does our God have a plan in all this? Do the Holy Scriptures reveal what His plan is for this gathering of wealth? As we *travel* farther, we will continue to examine the Scriptures and attempt to answer from the Holy Bible.

The first thing we must note is that our God has always, is now, and will forever be looking for those who will serve and obey Him. It is no different in this particular case. Notice in Exodus 4:22-23, as God is commissioning Moses to return to Egypt, He states: "And thou shalt say unto Pharaoh, Thus saith the LORD, Israel is my son, even my firstborn: And I say unto thee, Let my son go, that he may serve me: and if thou refuse to let him go, behold, I will slay thy son, even thy firstborn."

We notice in Exodus Chapter 11 that this is fulfilled. How amazing that the same judgment which killed the firstborn of Egypt had no effect on the firstborn of Israel! What made the difference? **Blood!** Notice Exodus 12:12-13:

> For I will pass through the land of Egypt this night, and will smite **all** of the firstborn in the land of Egypt, both man and beast; and against **all** the gods of Egypt I will execute judgment: I Am the LORD. And **the blood** shall be to you for a token upon the houses where ye are: and **when I see the blood, I will pass over you,** and the plague shall not be upon you to destroy you, when I smite the land of Egypt [emphasis mine].

Keeping in mind that God had told Pharaoh He wanted His people, Israel, to serve Him, we will examine this **service** and show how this was to involve the **wealth of Egypt.**

In Exodus 12:29-36, we see Pharaoh expelling Moses and the children of Israel out of the land of Egypt after the death of his firstborn. We read Verses 35-36:

> And the children of Israel did according to the words of Moses; and they **borrowed** of the Egyptians **jewels of silver, and jewels of gold, and raiment:** And the LORD gave the people **favor in the sight of the Egyptians,** so that they **lent** unto them such things as they required. **And they spoiled the Egyptians** [emphasis mine].

We must note that the Israelites took **three particular things: gold, silver, raiment**, just as God had previously instructed Moses to do. Why? I feel God had a particular purpose in this spoil as we shall try to show later. Also, it is for sure that the children of Israel took many other things that are not mention in these particular verses. We can see the evidence of this in Exodus Chapter 25 when at Moses' request Israel brings a variety of materials with which to build the tabernacle in the wilderness (More on this, shortly.)

This spoiling mentioned in Exodus 12:36 is very notable, because in Exodus Chapter 25 we begin to see one of the reasons for this **gathering of wealth in Egypt**. One thing is for sure: Anyone who has gone on tours through this wilderness, as I have, is very much aware these Israelites did not gather this wealth while traveling through the wilderness of Sinai. That being the case, I would think God had the pharaohs of four centuries gather up this massive **wealth, beginning with Joseph**. Then, from the effects of what Joseph instituted—one-fifth for Pharaoh and four-fifths for the people.

Once again, I would like to respectfully add that Joseph gave the Egyptians a better deal than most of us Americans get from the federal government on our income tax rate. I have paid as high as thirty-five percent, which is over one-third of my wages in tax. By the way, have you ever met anyone who just loved to pay taxes to the government? Well, with the hundreds of billions being given away by our government, they will probably have a blast in the next few decades. It takes taxpayers a while to pay off hundreds of billions!

Added note: While I have been involved in the completion of this manuscript, these billions have turned into trillions! May God have mercy on America!

We will now move into the wilderness of Sinai and examine the building of the tabernacle in Exodus 25:1-8 and see if this will add validity to our position. We read:

> And the LORD spake unto Moses, saying, Speak unto the children of Israel, that they bring **me** an offering: Of every man that giveth it willingly with his heart ye shall take **my offering**. And this is the offering which ye shall take of them; gold, and silver, and brass, And blue, and purple, and scarlet, and fine linen, and goats' hair, And rams' skins died red, and badgers' skins, and shittim wood, Oil for the light, spices

for anointing oil, and for sweet incense, Onyx stones, and stones to be set in the ephod, and in the breastplate. **And let them make me a sanctuary; that I may dwell among them** [emphasis mine].

Please note: In these Scriptures, God refers to the wealth gathered in Egypt (from the time of Joseph, to the deliverance of Israel by Moses into Sinai), as "**My offering.**"

After over four hundred years of acquiring **wealth** through the mighty Pharaohs of Egypt, I truly believe we can see the initial purpose in the mind of God: **That Israel might make their God a sanctuary on Earth in which He could "dwell among them."**

The last time we read of God dwelling on earth among His people is in Genesis 3:8. We read: "And they heard the voice of the LORD God **walking in the garden in the cool of the day**: And Adam and his wife hid themselves from the presence of the Lord God amongst the trees of the garden.

A short time later, we hear the LORD God speak in Genesis 3:22-23: "And the LORD God said, Behold, the man is become as one of **us**, to know good and evil: and now, lest he put forth his hand, and take also of the tree of life, and eat, and live for ever: Therefore the LORD God sent him forth from the garden of Eden, to till the ground from whence he was taken."

Ussher's Chronology of the Bible dates Genesis Chapter 3 at about 4004 B.C. As we have already seen, this is about the time when Adam and his wife, Eve, were expelled from the physical presence of God and **lost the First Eden.** This same *Ussher's Chronology* dates Exodus Chapter 25 at about 1491 B.C. This would suggest it had been approximately 2,513 years since God had personally come down to a designated place of communion with His creation on Planet Earth. **It sounds like God is preparing for a change of residence!**

Although, the Bible gives reference to Enoch and Noah walking with God, contextually I have not found any indication God came to Earth and **dwelt** with these men in their person. That is not the case in Exodus 25:8. Israel's God is now ready to come and **dwell among** them. It seems God is excited, but we must note: God will not evidently come to just any tabernacle. He is very careful to tell Moses he must make it and all the instruments after the pattern God had shown Moses on the mount.

Note: How could some people have pre-conceived ideas that the LORD would never set His feet on this sinful Earth? It seems to me the Holy Scriptures teach that Israel's God could hardly wait to come down and dwell with His people in this wilderness on Planet Earth! With these instructions (given in the middle of the desert to expelled slaves), it would be evident that most, if not all, of these materials would have been acquired in Egypt (one of the most sinful nations of that day) and brought to this present destination. It also seems evident that Israel's God not only **permitted but helped to orchestrate** all of the events recorded thus far, covering hundreds of years, in order that this vast stockpile of **wealth** might arrive in the desert **on Planet Earth** right on time. Whether some "super religious" people like it or not, God will do with His people as He pleases.

Remember, the super religious people in Jesus' day did not believe that Jehovah God *had come* to Earth in the person of Jesus Christ. Jesus had some very harsh words for those Pharisee and Sadducee doubters. Amen.

Now, back to our subject.

When I think of the gold alone required to build the tabernacle, make the ark, make a mercy seat, overlay a table of shittim wood, make the candlesticks, make the fifty taches, make the five hanging pillars and their hooks, make the alter of incense, make the breastplate, make the golden bells, make the golden plate, overlay the house of boards, make the wreathen chains, etc., it staggers my imagination! In all this, I have only mentioned the components overlaid with gold. If we read in God's Word, all the things required to build this tabernacle for God to come down and dwell with Israel, the list would also include silver, brass, precious stones of all kinds, rams' skins, badgers' skins, and other things too numerous to mention. It would be easy, to think that God used all the wealth Israel had brought from Egypt, but a careful study of Exodus 32:1-4 will reveal quite a different story.

Here, we see an impatient and faithless Israel demanding that Aaron make them gods like unto the gods of Egypt. To say the least, there was ample gold to make these molten images like unto a calf. We hear the Israelites say in **Exodus 32:4b:** "... These be thy gods, O Israel, which brought thee up out of the land of Egypt."

So, it is easy to see there was ample wealth left in the individual Israelites' possessions. This is well demonstrated in Exodus 36:5-7. We read:

> And they spake unto Moses, saying, The people bring **much more than enough** for the service of the work which the LORD commanded to make. And Moses gave commandment, and they caused it to be proclaimed throughout the camp, saying, Let neither man nor woman make any more work for the offering of the sanctuary. So the people were **restrained from bringing.** For the **stuff** they had was sufficient for all the work to make it, **and too much** [emphasis mine].

There is no doubt this gold, silver, and wealth in general brought from Egypt remained with this Israelite society as they journeyed into the land of Canaan, even though all of the people over twenty years old died in the wilderness for their unbelief at Kadesh-barnea.

This Kadesh-barnea is the place where the ten spies that did not believe God gave the bad report that there were **giants** in this land of Canaan (Numbers 13:26-33). Many believe these giants were the result of a second invasion of fallen angels cohabiting with women on Earth after the flood. Remember, Deuteronomy 3:11 where (depending on what cubit you use—either eighteen or twenty-one inches) Og had a bed thirteen to fifteen feet long and five and a half to seven feet wide. Think about it again, my friend: **That sure is a lot of bed!**

Now, let's get back to God gathering **His wealth.**

I cannot imagine all the wealth required for such an endeavor. It is for sure only the Lord God of all creation could have orchestrated such a massive acquisition of wealth over a period of over four hundred years and brought to pass its transfer from the Egyptians to the Israelite slaves in Goshen. And then later, by His mighty sovereign power, raise up Moses to lead these hundreds of thousands of Hebrew slaves into the Sinai Desert and bring them to this point in time into the land He had promised!

I know of no other recorded endeavor to gather wealth up to this time such as is recorded here in Genesis and Exodus. This just might be one of the greatest miracles in all the Old Testament.

What was on the mind of God as He brought into being and orchestrated this wealth acquisition?

Answer to question #3 on page 98:

Simply, to build Himself a house to come down and dwell with His people, Israel, on Earth (Exodus 25:8,22).

As we follow these Israelites through Scripture, we see them go through many trials and tribulations because of their unbelief and murmuring, but, as always, our God fulfills His promise and they finally enter the land promised to them under the leadership of Joshua.

A large number of religious people are still asking today: Why would God take so much notice to this particular group of people called Jews? We hear Moses give the answer in the Holy Words of God in Deuteronomy 7:6b–10. We read:

> ... The LORD thy God has chosen thee [Israel] to be a special people unto himself, above all people that are upon the face of the earth. The LORD did not set his love upon you, nor choose you, because you were more in number than any people; for ye were the fewest of all people; But because the LORD loved you, and **because he would keep the oath that he had sworn unto your fathers,** hath the LORD brought you out with a mighty hand, and redeemed you out of the house of bondmen, from the hand of Pharaoh king of Egypt. Know therefore that the LORD thy God, he is God, the Faithful God, which keepeth covenant and mercy with them that love him and keep his commandments **to a thousand generations;** And repayeth them that hate him to their face, to destroy them: he will not be slack to him that hateth him, he will repay him to his face [emphasis and commentary mine].

It is easy to see that God is only keeping His Word which He gave to Abraham, the father of this Nation of Israel.

However, just because Israel has entered the Promised Land, this is by no means the end of God's plan to acquire wealth in the Earth. As stated before, this gathering of wealth continues into The Last Eden where we view the pure gold New Jerusalem, eternal home of the married wife of Jesus Christ! (See Revelation 21:9–10.) More on this subject in Chapters Six through Eight.

When this Nation of Israel enters the Promised Land, we

are not told if the prior inhabitants of the land were wealthy in gold, silver, and precious stones, etc. even though we are told these things did exist. The Bible simply says that this Promised Land was a land flowing with milk and honey.

In our mind, we think of milk and honey as being symbols of a bountiful food source, not acquired wealth such as gold, silver, and precious stones. Also, when Joshua, Caleb, and the ten other spies returned from spying out the land, I recall no record in Scripture where they brought back precious metals. However, other Scriptures give evidence there were precious metals in the land.

One thing we can know, for sure: this gold, silver, and wealth in general brought from Egypt remained with this Israelite society as they journeyed into the Promised Land, even though all of the people over 20 years old died for their unbelief in the wilderness at Kadesh–barnea. Once again, we must remember that this Kadesh–barnea is the place where ten of the twelve spies **did not believe God**. They gave a bad report because they feared the mighty giants in the land of Cannan. We read in Numbers 13:33: "And there we saw the **giants, the sons of Anak,** which come of the giants: and **we were in our own sight as grasshoppers, and so we were in their sight.**"

After forty years of wandering in the wilderness of Sinai (forty being the Biblical number of testing[24]), we see Joshua in his final conquest of the land of Canaan destroying these satanic nations of mighty giant's who were descendants of Ham. As we have shown, Satan had hoped to use these ungodly peoples to destroy the **promised seed** of Israel through whom would be born the Savior of the world, but ultimately failed.

We read in Joshua 11:14,18,21–23:

---

24. Hutchings, *Master Mathematician*

And all the spoil of these cities, and the cattle, the children of Israel took for a prey unto themselves; but **every man** they smote with the edge of the sword, until they had destroyed them, **neither left they any to breathe.** . . . Joshua made war a long time with all those kings. . . . And at that time came Joshua, and cut off the Anakims from the mountains, from Hebron, from Debir, from Anab, and from **all** the mountains of Judah, and from **all** the mountains of Israel: **Joshua destroyed them utterly with their cities.** There was **none** of the Anakims [Canaanite giants who descended from Ham[25]] left in the land of the children of Israel: only in **Gaza,** in **Gath,** and in **Ashdod,** there remained. **So Joshua took the whole land,** according to all that the LORD said unto Moses; and Joshua gave it for an inheritance unto Israel according to their divisions by their tribes. **And the land rested from war** [emphasis and commentary mine].

We also notice back in Joshua 6:19,24 that as the people of Israel are marching around the city of Jericho. Joshua is instructed by God to put all the **silver, gold,** and vessels of **brass** and **iron** taken from this sinful city (after it's destruction) into the treasury of the house of the Lord.

We have already learned what God probably has in mind for this wealth, whatever the amount, have we not?

As we travel on to the Books of First and Second Samuel, we see the people of Israel unsatisfied with God's plan of prophet-priest in the great man, Samuel. In this time of Israel's history, when Samuel's sons walked not in the ways of their father but walked after filthy lucre, took bribes, and perverted judgment, the people of Israel cry out to Samuel to make them a king to reign over the nation.

---

25. Strong, *Exhaustive Concordance*

We hear the LORD God speak on this matter to Samuel the prophet in 1 Samuel 8:7. We read: "And the LORD said unto Samuel, Hearken unto the voice of the people in all that they say unto thee: for they have not rejected thee, but they have rejected me, that I should not reign over them."

I am very concerned that our country has reached this point in history, which, as it did for Israel, can only end in judgment.

In this time of unrest among the people of Israel, God permits Saul to be chosen king. Saul was a choice man and goodly. He stood from his shoulders and upward higher than any other man in Israel. But, as kings, presidents, and prime ministers often do, Saul became self-willed and was rejected by the God of Israel when he would not wait on the prophet Samuel's advice at Michmash. We read in 1 Samuel 13:14: "But now thy kingdom shall not continue: The LORD hath sought him a man after his own heart, and the LORD hath commanded him to be captain over his people, **because thou hast not kept that which the LORD commanded thee."**

The particular man Samuel was making reference to you will find noted in 1 Samuel 16:1: "And the LORD said unto Samuel, How long wilt thou mourn for Saul, seeing I have rejected him from reigning over Israel? fill thy horn with oil, and go, I will send thee to Jesse the Beth-lehemite: for I have provided **me** a king among his sons."

This causes Samuel to be very afraid because of Saul's wrath. God instructs Samuel to take an heifer for a sacrifice and say: "I am come to sacrifice to the Lord." As the sacrifice was in process, Samuel had Jesse to bring his sons before him. Jesse brought seven of his sons and God rejected **all seven**. We continue to read 1 Samuel 16:11-13:

And Samuel said unto Jesse, Are here all thy children?

> And he said, There remaineth yet the youngest, [**number eight**[26]] and, behold, he keepeth the sheep. And Samuel said unto Jesse, Send and fetch him: for we will not sit down till he come hither. And he sent, and brought him in. Now he was ruddy, and withal of a beautiful countenance, and goodly to look to. **And the LORD said, Arise, anoint him: for this is he.** Then Samuel took the horn of oil, and anointed him in the midst of his brethren: **and the Spirit of the LORD came upon David from that day forward.** So Samuel rose up, and went to Ramah [emphasis mine].

In this act of anointing David to be king over Israel and the Spirit of God coming upon him from that day forward, we now see **a new beginning of wealth acquisition** as David takes the kingdom from Saul. He begins to gather **wealth** from all the regions, in order **to build God a house for His namesake. This house would not be in the wilderness but at Jerusalem.**

Just as King David is going to fulfill his dream of building God a house for God to come down and commune with His people, Israel, he is attacked by the devil and commits a very grave sin with Bathsheba, wife of Uriah the Hittite. This act, along with the issue of warring with the many enemies of Israel, would, ultimately, cost King David the privilege of building God's house, **but not the privilege of continuing to gather massive amounts of wealth for that purpose.**

Note: I assure you King David is no different from you and I in this respect; working hard for the LORD will usually bring an attack from the Devil. We **must** guard our lives when we are under the blessings of God. The old devil is good at giving us the **"big head."** It worked on King David, and, my friend, it has

---

26. Hutchings, *Master Mathematician*

worked many times since! Many are the men and women who have wandered from their God-ordained mates because the old devil painted a false picture in their minds. **Green grass grows best in the will of God, not on the other side of the fence!** AMEN.

After he and Bathsheba are married, they have a son born named Solomon. This Solomon would eventually grow to become heir of David's throne and be anointed king of Israel. Solomon would take all the **wealth** which King David had acquired and add much more **wealth** to build the most magnificent **temple** for the LORD in the history of the world. But this did not happen by chance. In his youth Solomon prayed to God and asked for wisdom to judge God's people, Israel, in 1 Kings 3:7-13. We read:

> And now, O LORD my God, Thou hast made Thy servant king instead of David my father: and I am but a little child: I know not how to go out or come in. And thy servant is in the midst of thy people which thou hast chosen, a great people, that cannot be numbered nor counted for multitude. Give therefore thy servant an understanding heart to judge thy people; that I may discern between good and bad: for who is able to judge this thy so great a people? **And the speech pleased the LORD**, that Solomon had asked this thing. And God said unto him, Because thou hast asked this thing, and hast not asked for thyself long life; **neither hast asked riches for thyself**, nor hast asked the life of thy enemies; but hast asked for thyself understanding to discern judgment; Behold, **I have done according to thy words:** lo, I have given thee a wise and an understanding heart; so that there was none like thee before thee, neither after thee shall any arise like unto thee. And I have also given thee that which thou

hast not asked, **both riches, and honour:** so that there shall not be any among the kings like unto thee all thy days [emphasis mine].

First Kings 4:29 continues: "And God gave Solomon wisdom and understanding exceeding much, and largeness of heart, even as the sand that is on the sea shore."

In 1 Kings 5:13,15-16), we read of the massive manpower involved in the construction of this house **for God to come down and dwell with His people, Israel.** We read:

> And king Solomon raised a levy out of all Israel; and the levy was thirty thousand men. . . . And Solomon had threescore and ten thousand that bare burdens, and fourscore thousand hewers in the mountains; Beside the chief of Solomon's officers which were over the work, three thousand and three hundred, which ruled over the people that wrought in the work.

This gives a grand total of 183,300 workers, besides the men not mentioned in number that Hiram, king of Tyre, sent with King Solomon's men to this work.

It is not known nor can it be found, the amount of gold, silver, brass, and other precious things Solomon acquired and put into the **House of the Lord** in order for **God, Himself, to come down and commune with His people, Israel.**

In like manner, neither tongue nor pin could tell what Our God has in store for the **wealth lying-in-wait** on Planet Earth. However, before we leave Chapter Five, I would like to look at a few Scriptures that might shed some light on God's **future acquisitions and intentions** between now and **The Last Eden.**

Note: Folks, why don't we just admit that the wonder and excitement of prophecy is simply this: God saw history in advance, and then He had His holy men of old (through the Holy Spirit) write it down for you and I to discern and expound (as it is written). Past history, then, has proven past prophecies in God's Word to be true. Also, present prophecy is informing us of future history. If you and I want to know the future, we need to read the Holy Bible, not the newspaper or something seen in the media. Media certainly has its place, but not as a discerner of God's Holy Scriptures. According to God's Word, only saved, born-again believers can discern the Holy Scriptures. **(Read 1 Corinthians 2:14; 12:3; 2 Peter 1:19-21; and Revelation 1:1,19.)**

Now, back to God's future acquisitions.

As we look in Daniel 11:28a, we see the future Antichrist in the process of consolidating his kingdom. We read: "... Then shall he [the Antichrist] return into his land with **great riches**; and his heart shall be against the holy covenant."

Also, Daniel 11:43a reads: "... But he [the Antichrist) shall have power over the **treasuries of gold and of silver**, and over **all** of the **precious things of Egypt.**"

Note: Since the Antichrist will have dominion over the entire planet, I would assume he will also have the power to gather wealth from the entire world. This just may be in process in November of 2008 as I sit in my study and work on this manuscript. In the past four to five weeks we have seen what I believe could be a "created" international banking crisis. The reason I say this crisis could be created is that all these nations' financial systems fell into disarray at one time! So, these international bankers could be at work already! However, as we move forward to go **Beyond the Revelation**, as we have already noted, God's saints need not worry. All such labors will turn to benefit the LORD and His married wife (remember Revelation 19:7-8)!

Keeping this in mind, Micah 4:13 gives this Verse just

prior to the Battle of Armageddon: "Arise and thresh, O daughter of Zion: for I will make thy horn iron, and I will make thy hoofs brass: and thou shalt beat in pieces many people: and *I will* **consecrate their** *gain* **unto the** LORD, **and their** *substance* **unto the** LORD *of the whole earth."*

I wonder what Our God will do with all of this gain and substance. But, then, we really know. Don't we? **Remember, the** LORD**'s true church are joint (equal) heirs with Jesus.**

During the battle recorded in Zechariah 14, Verse 14 gives this information: "And Judah also shall fight at Jerusalem; and the **wealth of** *all* **the heathen round about shall be gathered together, gold, and silver, and apparel in great abundance."** Notice, the Scripture says wealth of **"all"** the heathen. That, surely, will be a bunch of wealth. Also, notice: These are the exact same items that were brought out of Egypt—**gold, silver, and apparel.** What do you think God has in mind? It just might be a **latter house.** Let's read Haggai and see:

> For thus saith the LORD of hosts; yet once, it is a little while, and I will shake the **heavens**, and the **earth**, and the sea, and the **dry land**; And I will **shake all nations**, and the **desire of all nations** shall come: **and I will fill** *this house* **with glory** saith the LORD of hosts. **The silver is mine, and the gold is mine, saith the** LORD **of hosts.** The **glory** of this **latter house** shall be greater than of the former, saith the LORD of hosts; and **in this place will I give peace,** saith the LORD of hosts.
>
> —Haggai 2:6–9 [emphasis mine]

Haggai is careful to let God's saints know our Holy God will still be gathering wealth (gold and silver) in the last days, because He is building this **latter house** at Jerusalem for the Millennial Kingdom. Hallelujah!

Isaiah 60:9,13, 17 gives more insight on future wealth acquisitions:

> Surely the isles shall wait for **me**, and the ships of Tarshish first, to bring thy sons from far, their **silver** and their **gold** with them, **unto the name of the LORD thy God, and to the Holy One of Israel**, because He hath glorified thee... . The **glory of Lebanon shall come unto thee**, the fir tree, the pine tree, and the box together, **to beautify the place of my Sanctuary; and I will make the place of my** *feet* **glorious**. . . . For brass **I will** bring **gold**, and for iron **I will** bring **silver**, and for wood brass, and for stones iron: **I will** also make thy officers peace, and thy exactors righteousness [emphasis mine].

Surely, we have given enough evidence to show **why** our God has allowed acquiring **wealth** down through the ages and still doing so today. He has permitted men to gather this **wealth,** then orchestrated its use for Himself, in order that He might have a house to come down and dwell on this Earth with His creation, **Adam/man.**

In Zechariah 6:12-13, we see this final House of God (on this Earth), the Millennial temple being built by Christ Jesus, Himself! We read:

> And speak unto him, saying, Thus speaketh the LORD of hosts, saying, Behold the man whose name is **The BRANCH;** and he shall grow up out of his place, and **he shall build the temple of The LORD:** Even he shall build the **temple of the LORD**; and **he shall bear the glory**, and shall **sit and rule upon** *his throne;* and **he shall be a priest upon** *his throne:* and the **counsel of peace** shall be between them both [emphasis mine].

Also, read Luke 1:31-33.

We feel positive this man whose name is The **BRANCH** is in no way making reference to Joshua in Zechariah 6:11; but is making reference to Jesus Christ in Verse 13 as both King and Priest upon His throne (after the order of Melchisedec), with the counsel of peace between these two positions of Christ. (Carefully read Hebrews 7.)

I feel the evidence given in this Chapter is overwhelming in support of our God **gathering wealth** for the sole purpose of building Himself houses to **come to Earth** and dwell with His beloved creation—man! We might think the Millennium temple would be the last of these great temples which God would gather wealth to build. However, that is not the case.

As we move closer, to go **Beyond the Revelation**, Chapter Eight of this manuscript will take us beyond this present Heaven and Earth into the New Heaven and the New Earth. There, in **The Last Eden,** we will see a **fifteen hundred-mile cubed city made of pure gold, like unto clear glass! The wall around the city is of jasper. The foundations are garnished with all manner of precious stones. The twelve gates are twelve pearls, with every several gate being one pearl.**

When I read this description of the New Jerusalem, it sounds as if our God might have purified the wealth of all the ages and performed a carry-over (from this Earth to the New Earth) when this Earth was destroyed by consuming fire. When I consider a city (fifteen hundred miles cubed) made of pure gold, friend, that's a **lot of gold.**

However, He could have made a fifteen hundred miles cubed city of pure gold *from nothing.* After all, Jesus Christ is God incarnate!

But, we must not get ahead of ourselves, for we are now ready to move into Chapter Six where we ask the question:

Will the King be revealed? I would, certainly, think, in order to have a kingdom, we must have a King. With the momentum God has displayed in the past to build Himself a house, on Planet Earth, I would think He will continue this quest (through the two thousand-year Grace Dispensation) until He has finally accomplished His will, married Himself a wife, and moved to Planet Earth. Would you not think He would? We will see later that Revelation 19:7-9 (where His wife has made herself ready for this marriage and return to Planet Earth) is a prelude to this being *totally* fulfilled!

Remember: After the Rapture, wherever Jesus Christ moves, the Church moves (1 Thessalonians 4:17).

As we leave Chapter Five, **let's read a prelude Verse to Chapter Six: "And the Lord shall be king over all the *earth:* in that day shall there be one Lord, and his name one"** (Zechariah 14:9, emphasis mine).

In the words of a grand old Church Hymn: What a day that will be!

Now, let's move forward to Chapter Six.

Chapter Six

Will The King Be Revealed?

As we continue our *journey,* I remember years ago in the 1960s, I began to examine the Words of the Living God on a particular prophetic subject. **The burden in my heart was: Will there be a physical revelation of God's blessed Son, Jesus Christ, on this Earth after the Grace Dispensation? And, if so, what will happen beyond that Revelation as related in the Holy Scriptures?**

This all came about because of an event happening one Sunday morning in September of 1967, as I was attending Sunday school in a little one-room Baptist church sanctuary which sits over oil and gas deposits on a rocky hillside in Middle Tennessee. This is the same small Baptist church sanctuary where I first heard the love of Jesus Christ for all humanity being preached by God's called ministers. In the 1970s, a new church sanctuary was built across the road in a much better location, and I still have my membership there today. It was in this small one-room sanctuary that my interest in the subject of Bible prophecy was magnified by the assignment of a project from the Book of Daniel.

My Sunday school teacher, a very well read man, was teaching his class with much sincerity this prophetic Book of Daniel. To my surprise, he assigned me the task of giving a report the following Sunday morning, the subject being: Daniel 2:34-35,44-45.

To an experienced Bible scholar, this might have seemed a small task; but to someone who had just started attending Sunday school one month earlier, and had never spent time in the Holy Scriptures as he should, it seemed an insurmountable task. The, only Bible Verses that I knew by memory were John 11:35 and Psalms 23.

I can't remember, the exact words I said the following Sunday morning, but I do remember one thing: These four Verses of Scripture from Daniel Chapter 2 **forever changed my life.** They propelled me into a lifetime of interest and study that has continued until this day.

Very early in this Christian experience, I realized that in order for Jesus Christ to be revealed as King and have a universal Kingdom over all the Earth, there are a number of things that must first exist:

1. First, there must be a man, **one man,** who can qualify for this position.
2. That same man must have the **power and resources** to execute his dominion and influence over the whole realm of peoples and nations of Planet Earth.
3. The **prophetic timing** of the ages must be in place for these events to come to pass (what God saw and had His holy prophets pen in Scripture).
4. Mankind, as a whole, **must become willing** for this to take place, even if it means this willingness is accomplished by force (see Revelation 19:11-21; 20:1-6).

Daniel prophesied in Daniel 2:34-35,44-45 of such a **man** when he wrote these prophetic words which God used to introduce me to His Holy Bible. We read:

> Thou sawest till that **a stone was cut out without hands**, which smote the image upon **his feet** that were of iron and clay, and brake them to pieces. **Then** was the iron, the clay, the brass, the silver, and the gold, **broken to pieces "together,"** and became like the chaff [see Isaiah 41:8–16] of the summer threshing floors; and the wind carried them away, **that no place was found for them:** and **the stone that smote the image became a great mountain [or kingdom], and filled the whole earth.** . . . **And in the days of these kings** [the smitten kings that could no longer be found, *chaff*] shall the God of heaven **set up a kingdom,** which shall **never** be destroyed: and the kingdom shall not be left to other people, but **it [the kingdom that is set up]** shall break in pieces and **consume all these kingdoms, and it shall stand for ever.** Forasmuch as thou sawest that **the stone** was cut out of the mountain **without hands,** and that **it [the stone]** break in pieces the iron, the brass, the clay, the silver and the gold; The Great God hath made known to the king what shall come to pass hereafter: and the dream is certain, and the interpretation thereof sure [emphasis and commentary mine].

In the past six thousand years, many men and women (as kings, queens, presidents, prime ministers, etc.) have had limited success in reigning for different periods of time. As we look back through the history of this world, we see all those past rulers have one thing in common. Though some reigned for long periods of time and some for short periods of time, ultimately they all met this same grim fate. **They died**. It matters not if these rulers were on the side of the Lord God, or if they served the devil to the fullest; their kingdoms all eventually were cut short of total world dominion. If we only knew the statistics, I imagine many rulers went to an early grave by some unnatural means.

Do the Holy Scriptures speak of a time when the Words of God's holy prophets will be fulfilled concerning a worldwide kingdom run exclusively by one man? Different beliefs exist (as I soon learned back in 1967).

I also began to examine the Holy Scriptures to see if all of the references concerning this coming Kingdom were only spiritual and **already fulfilled in the death, burial and resurrection of Jesus Christ,** as some wanted me to believe. I wanted to know if there really would be a **literal fulfillment** of this promised Kingdom, on a **literal throne** of David, in a **literal city** called Jerusalem, on this **literal planet** called Earth.

Remembering Daniel 2:34-35, 44-45: I wanted to know if every kingdom on Planet Earth **had already been smitten** and become like the chaff of the summer threshing floor; and the wind **already carried them all away,** and **no place could be found for them.** As God as my witness: It does not seem logical to me that these things have **already** happened!

But as I soon found out that many people do not believe in a coming world kingdom run exclusively *first* by the Antichrist then by Jesus Christ.

Over these forty-plus years of study in the prophetic Word, I have attempted to not be so much interested in what man said about this matter (even though God's men and women have been *at times* both a help and a hindrance). Through all my discussions (though sometimes discouraged) I have attempted to *only* believe what God's Words has to say.

In the past, I have heard preachers and lay members of the Lord's church ridiculing this doctrine of Christ's Revelation and His reign over all the Earth quite often while never giving one single word of applicable Scripture to support their harsh claim. How terribly sad!

If you believe and preach John 3:16 as the pure Words of

God, why deny the prophecy of Daniel 2:34-35, 44-45? Where do we get the authority to select what we choose to believe and reject the rest?

I truly believe that if we are going to teach what God said, we should be more than happy to tell those to whom we speak **(from Scripture)** where God said what He said!

It is very difficult for me to believe God the Father would preserve this promised seed for four thousand years; let His Son be born (God incarnate) through that seed; live for over thirty-three years on this Earth; die for my sins and the sins of the whole world; rise from the grave and ascend back to God the Father, and yet never let Him be revealed to take His rightful place on the throne of David (as prophesied) to receive His well-deserved glory for one thousand years before He destroys this Earth, sin, and the devil for all eternity! (Read Revelation 20:1-15).

Let's read Luke 1:31-33. Here we find the angel speaking to Mary concerning the Son of God whom the Holy Ghost will soon conceive in her womb.

> And, behold, thou [the virgin Mary] shalt conceive in thy womb, and bring forth a son, and shalt call his name JESUS. He shall be great, and shall be called the Son of the Highest: **and the Lord God shall give unto him the throne of his father David: And he shall reign over the house of Jacob for ever;** and of **his kingdom** there shall be no end [emphasis mine].

Some say Jesus is already seated on David's throne in Heaven. I'm sorry, but the throne where Jesus is seated belongs to His Father, Jehovah God. David never had anything but an earthly throne. Any honest Christian who reads their Bible knows this.

I often wonder what people who decry the coming Kingdom will tell the Lord Jesus Christ when they are brought before Him at the Judgment Seat of Christ. Then I remember that many Christians who do not believe in Christ's coming Kingdom do not believe in a Judgment Seat of Christ either! (Read Romans 14:10 and 2 Corinthians 5:10.)

Picking and choosing what we believe when we read the Word of God has never been something I could understand in the Christian world.

If Jesus said that we will be "*caught up* to meet him in the air, and so shall we ever be with the LORD," I would think it would be easy to see that the remaining portions of the Bible (after the Rapture) would involve **Jesus and His church together!** Wouldn't you think it would?

You see, it is so simple that no one need be confused. The order of the future is **Rapture; then Revelation.**

The Bible makes it very clear that every person on Planet Earth has a future *somewhere*. I am satisfied in knowing that where Jesus Christ is, I will forevermore be. However, my satisfaction in knowing I will be with Jesus Christ forever (after the Rapture) does not in any way prove the validity of Scripture on the subject of His coming Kingdom and beyond. Only the Word of the True and Living God, contained in the Holy Scriptures, will give us the knowledge we need on this matter!

The Word of God plainly declare that this Jewish carpenter named Jesus Christ, who is God incarnate, will someday come down to the air and call His espoused bride up to meet Him, and from that very second, for all eternity, we will (bodily) be with Him and be like Him. Hallelujah!!!

Read 1 John 3:1-3.

We will now *move* farther into God's prophetic Scriptures and see if our Holy God has anything more to say about this subject of **the King being revealed.**

In the realm of religious people, you can find many different interpretations of what the Word of God teaches. Our subject in this Chapter on the coming Revelation and Kingdom of Jesus Christ is not any different in the respect that many differ on how the Scriptures teach this will unfold in the future.

Some believe that when Jesus Christ comes in the air for His espoused bride, He will **"zap" Planet Earth** and this will be the end of the matter.

Others believe that when Jesus Christ comes, He will **take up a continued presence *in* or *around* Planet Earth** until His purpose in prophecy is accomplished.

Still others believe that the church is going to **preach the Gospel, convert the world to Christ, and then invite Jesus Christ back to Earth.**

The list is endless as to what **people believe** concerning the Revelation of our Lord Jesus Christ and beyond.

With this in mind, it is not my intent in this Chapter to try to offend anyone with opposing views, but to present my views "for your consideration" on Christ's coming Kingdom as I see them (according to the Holy Scriptures).

It has taken six thousand years of God battling Satan to get us to this point of the King being revealed and, in my opinion, my Holy God is not going to let someone who just happens not to believe it stop Him from revealing Jesus Christ as King of Kings and Lord of Lords on Planet Earth!

After all, if everyone would be honest we should *all* ask ourselves: Where are the **kings** located over whom Jesus will be **King? Where are the lords located over whom Jesus will be Lord? In the timeframe of this particular Prophecy, they are all located on this Earth, the very place God put Adam in the beginning!**

As previously noted in this manuscript, the Holy Bible in Zechariah 14:9 makes it crystal clear: **The L**ORD **shall be King over "all the earth": in that day shall there be one Lord,**

and His Name one. (As far as I know, this planet is the only Earth there is).

God stopped Satan in his demonic invasion in Noah's day because Noah found grace in the eyes of the LORD and Noah was perfect in his generations. Even though God waited one hundred twenty years for man to repent, judgment finally came and it came as it has every time since—swiftly! In the future, there will be an Armageddon! God's patience does run out.

If we were to count the number of unfulfilled prophetic Scriptures on this subject of the coming Kingdom, there would be many. As we *move* forward in Chapter Six, we shall see more of these Scriptures and examine them **as they are written.**

In doing so, I feel we can easily establish that a coming Kingdom (on Earth) is taught in the Word of the living God and all signs point to it being very soon! However, I believe we must keep in mind that before this coming earthly Kingdom can be established, there will many predicted events of Scripture take place **in their Scriptural order.**

1. The **Rapture of the Church,** which will end the Grace Dispensation (1 Thessalonians 4:13-18).
2. **The Judgment Seat of Christ** some time prior to the coronation of the King (Romans 14:10-12; 2 Corinthians 5:10).
3. The **Coronation of the King** just prior to the awful wrath of God beginning on Planet Earth (Revelation 5:5-13).
4. The **Wrath of God on the Earth below** as given in the Revelation 6-18.
5. The **Marriage of the Lamb** after God's pre-war bombardment of the Antichrist and his physical and religious Babylon systems (Revelation 19:1-10).
6. Then, the **King** of all kings and **Lord** of all lords **"will be revealed"** to Planet Earth in full-scale war (to prevent the

Antichrist from totally destroying the Nation of Israel), at Armageddon (Revelation 19:11-21; Zechariah 14:1-5; Revelation 12:17).

7. Then, after a predicted number of days (Daniel 12:12), the **One Thousand-Year Kingdom Dispensation will begin** (Daniel 2:35; Ezekiel 47:1-12; Zechariah 14:8-9; Revelation 20:1-6; etc.).

We have walked through Scripture and have come to this time in our text to show that Christ Jesus, our Lord and Savior, will indeed be revealed to Planet Earth *moving* **Beyond His Revelation** and working His will on this planet for one thousand glorious years. This is the passion of this work and of my heart, even though (as we have seen) it all began in Genesis Chapter 1.

Let us not forget, as noted in this manuscript, that since the Garden of Eden, Satan has attempted to rule this world through his lackeys (both religious and secular). He has used anyone who would bend and bow to his will. But (as before stated) to this present day, I know of no one person who has been successful in accomplishing a world kingdom in which they could boast of world dominion under the rule of one individual, even though many have tried and some have come very close.

I am confident this will change in the not-too-distant future, as an ungodly world system is looming on the horizon! Everything we see today has come together, is coming together, or is making plans to merge in the future! Presidents, prime ministers, and dictators are merging; religions are merging; banks are merging; corporations are merging; nations are merging; systems of identification are merging; financial markets are merging. I would think someone would stand up and ask the appropriate question: **Why is everything coming to-**

gether?

I feel the only answer the Holy Bible gives is that a false one-world ruler is soon coming on the world scene whom the Scriptures call "that horn" in Daniel 7:20, "that antichrist" in 1 John 2:18, and "beast" in Revelation 13:1-10. This superman is going to arise and have dominion over the Earth for three and a half years (Revelation 13:5), just prior to the real Christ being revealed from Heaven with all of His Saints, in flaming fire (2 Thessalonians 1:8), in judgment upon all (Jude Verses 14-15), in total destruction of this beast and his kingdom (Revelation 19:11-21).

Then and only then has the "real" King, Jesus Christ, God's only Son, been revealed from Heaven. He will come to Planet Earth to reign for one thousand glorious years on the throne of His father David "from Jerusalem." Also read Isaiah 9:6b-7; 24:23; 62:1-7; 66:10-24, etc.)!

As we go farther into this great subject, I would like to look at the definition of this Bible word *"kingdom."* What exactly is the definition of a kingdom? Remember Isaiah 11:1-2 and Luke 1:31-33. The 1828 version of *Noah Webster's English Dictionary* defines "kingdom" in this manner: "**The territory or country subject to a king; the inhabitants or population subject to a king; government rule; supreme administration.**"

In *Strong's Concordance of the New Testament Greek Dictionary* it has one definition throughout the entire New Testament for the word "kingdom." It states: "**To rule; a realm of royalty.**"

In Old Testament Hebrew Scriptures (when referring to God's Kingdom), we find this Hebrew definition that *Strong's Exhaustive Concordance* has the same basic meaning given for the word "kingdom": "**dominion; realm; empire; royalty.**" The definition of "dominion" is "sovereign authority." So we see (from the available references of both Greek and Hebrew from which we get our English Bible) that they have the same definition of kingdom as we do in our *English Dictionary:* "**A realm; a dominion or empire of peoples ruled over by a king.**"

Note: With the definition of this word "kingdom" (from the English, Greek and Hebrew dictionaries) fresh in our minds, I would like to go on record as saying: The Kingdom of our God is not now, nor has it ever been, **within** a self-righteous, sinful human being. We should only have to look at the definition of the word "kingdom" to know this. However, let's look farther.

In Luke 17:21, we hear Jesus saying to these ungodly Pharisees: "Neither shall they say, Lo here! or, lo there! For, behold, the kingdom of God is **within you.**"

This particular Greek word translated into English **"within"** is *en-tos,* literally meaning "in the midst."[27] If we trace this Greek reference 1787 back to the root word *en* (Greek reference 1722), we discover its true meaning which is, "**about, against, among.**" If we will look back into Luke 17:20, we will hear Jesus talking to self-righteous, God-rejecting Pharisees. Jesus would never say to such people, "The Kingdom **(as to its spiritual content)** is inside you. However, the Kingdom was actually **"in the midst"** of the Pharisees in the persons of the King and His disciples as they walked in and around Jerusalem on Earth.

In New Testament Christianity, saved people are **born into the Kingdom of God by the new birth. Christ Jesus** comes into the converted individual. We read Colossians 1:27: "To whom God would make known what is the riches of the glory of this mystery among the Gentiles; which is **Christ in you,** the hope of glory." Christ Jesus (who is the Savior) is **in**

---

27. Strong, *Exhaustive Concordance*

every born-again believer **in the person of the Holy Ghost** and, according to the Scriptures, He will some day reign over His Kingdom on Earth!

In Acts 1:9, this same King, Jesus Christ (rejected by the Jewish Nation of Israel), left Planet Earth and was taken **up** to God's Throne.

At this present moment (7:41 p.m., July 22, 2009), there has been no Rapture. One way I know the Rapture has not happened is that I am presently sitting in my study typing on a 2000 version Dell computer keyboard. This being said, it is logical to assume He is still on the right hand of the Father! AMEN!

Added note: My 1996 Compact computer crashed on February 5, 2009, at 12:30 p.m. One pop and half this manuscript was gone. Thank God for hard copies and backup discs! If you see Satan, tell him: He is *still* a mean, dirty, lousy loser!

Now, back to Daniel.

As we look at these definitions of the word "Kingdom," we are immediately reminded of the Words our God gave us in Daniel Chapter 7. Here, God (in prophecy) is rehearsing over and over through eight Verses the issues of Jesus Christ and His Saints going **Beyond the Revelation** and **taking** the kingdoms of this world from the Antichrist (or beast). We will now read some of the most exciting Verses in all future prophecy—Daniel 7:9, 13-14, 18, 21-22, 26-28a:

> I beheld till **the thrones were *cast* down**, and the Ancient of days **did sit,** whose garment was white as snow, and the hair of his head like the pure wool; **his throne** was like the firey flame, and his wheels as the burning fire. . . . I saw in the night visions, and, behold, one like the **Son of Man** came *with* the clouds of heaven [read Revelation 1:7], and came to the Ancient of Days, and they brought him near before

him. **And there was given him dominion, and glory, and a kingdom, that all people, nations, and languages, should serve him:** His dominion is an everlasting dominion, which shall not pass away, and **his kingdom** that which shall not be destroyed.... [See also Revelation 5:7-10]. But the saints of the Most High shall **take the kingdom, and possess the kingdom for ever, even for ever, and ever.** ... I beheld, and the same horn [Beast] made war with the saints, and prevailed against them: **Until the Ancient of Days came, and judgment was given to the saints of the Most High; and the time came that the Saints possessed the kingdom.** ... But the **judgment** shall sit, and **they** [the saints] **shall take away his** [the beast's] **dominion,** to consume and to destroy it unto the end. And the kingdom and dominion and the greatness of the kingdom *under* **the whole heaven, shall be** *given* **to the people of the saints of the Most High, whose kingdom is an everlasting kingdom, and** *all dominions* **shall serve and obey him.** Hitherto, is the end of the matter ... [emphasis mine].

Wow! These future prophecies should take away our breath as we read and stand in awe of what our Holy King Jesus has in store for His Saints in the future.

As we can see from these Verses of future prophecy, Daniel declares the end of the matter! How, I pray, all fellow Christians would follow Daniel's lead and declare, "Hitherto is the end of the matter!"

How could anyone who has an open mind read these Verses in Daniel Chapter 7 and not understand: **The day is coming when Jesus Christ will be revealed and establish His Kingdom and reign over the entire Earth?** (See again Revelation 19:11-21; 20:1-6).

But in case we need greater understanding, let's go back

and review these Verses in Daniel Chapter 7 (and others) once more, with some comments.

Daniel 7:9 tells us the Ancient of Days did sit **after all other thrones had been cast down**. Hence, the physical return of Christ to fight the Battle of Armageddon. Daniel 7:14 lets us know this Ancient of Days was given dominion, glory, and a Kingdom in which **all** people, nations, and languages should serve Him. Also, we are told this dominion and kingdom **shall not be destroyed** (more on this subject in Chapter Eight). Daniel 7:18 informs us that **the Saints** will be involved in the **taking and possessing** of this Kingdom, but other Scriptures tells us that Saints will not fight at Armageddon (see Isaiah 63:1-6). Daniel 7:22 reveals how **judgment will be *given* to the Saints** of the Most High only after the Ancient of Days has come and conquered.

Let me insert here in 1 Corinthians 6:2-3 that the beloved Apostle Paul gives the church at Corinth a very important **companion prophecy** to Daniel 7:22. We read: "Do ye not know that **the Saints *shall* judge the world?** and if the world shall be judged **by you,** are ye unworthy to judge the smallest matters? Know ye not that **we *shall* judge angels?** how much more things that pertain to this life?"

Also, Revelation 20:4 gives us the total fulfillment of this 1 Corinthians 6:2-3 companion prophecy. We read: "And I saw thrones, and **they** sat upon them, and **judgment was given unto them:** and I saw the souls of them that were beheaded for the witness of Jesus, and for the Word of God, and which had not worshipped the beast, neither his image, neither had received his mark upon their foreheads, or in their hands; **and they lived and reigned with Christ a thousand years.** Sounds like the King is totally revealed to Planet Earth, doesn't it?

And now, back to Daniel Chapter 7:

Daniel 7:26-27 tells us of the destruction of the beast, his dominion destroyed, and the Kingdom and dominion **under the whole heaven** being turned over to **the Saints of the Most High.** This Kingdom is declared to be everlasting and **all dominions** shall serve and obey Him (Jesus Christ, the King).

We should not forget John wrote in Revelaticn 2:26-27 **"to the New Testament church at Thyatira"** this conformation of Daniel 7:27—power over all nations being given to the people of the Saints of the Most High. We read: "And he that overcometh, and keepeth my works unto the end, to him will I give **power over the nations; And he shall rule them with a rod of iron;** as the vessels of a potter shall they be **broken to shivers:** even as I received of my father."

Now, a good question at this point would be: "Is every person **under the whole Heaven** serving and obeying Jesus Christ in this present Dispensation of God's loving Grace?" I don't think so. Do you?

Do the Saints of God have total dominion over this planet at this present time, or is Satan running the show? I believe the answer is obvious.

Someone might say: *I don't understand how this could literally happen on Planet Earth.* I would lovingly say to such people, I don't understand how a virgin who has never known a man could literally have a baby named Jesus Christ on Planet Earth, but by the power of Almighty God, she did.

So, the Ancient of Days (Jesus Christ) is coming under the whole Heaven, and the only place I know that is under the whole Heaven is Planet Earth.

When the true Church leaves Earth in the Rapture, we go **up** through the first heaven (where birds fly), **through** the second heaven (where the planets are), **to** the third Heaven (the abode of God). **Up** in Rapture; **Down** in Revelation: It is that simple.

If this prophesied coming Kingdom is **under** the whole Heaven (Daniel 7:27), I believe the issue is pretty well settled by God in Daniel's writings, since the Holy Bible was written in retrospect to the people on Planet Earth, not some other place in the universe.

I hope I have already given sufficient Scripture to show a coming world Kingdom is prophesied by God's prophets. It will be established and administered on Planet Earth after or **Beyond the Revelation** of Jesus Christ and His Saints (Revelation 19:11–21).

However, I would like to go back and begin at the beginning, when God *first* promised to establish a Kingdom on Earth through a particular man. I would also like to bring to light some of the mighty acts God worked through His chosen people in order that the ultimate fulfillment of this promise could come to pass.

For the identity of this particular man, we will go back to the promises found in 2 Samuel 7:10–17, and view these great promises God our Father gave to King David *in future prophecy* over three thousand years ago. We read:

> Moreover I will appoint a place for **my people Israel,** and will plant them, that they may dwell **in a place of their own,** and **move no more;** neither shall the children of wickedness afflict them any more, as beforetime, And as since the time that I commanded judges to be over my people Israel, and have caused thee to rest from all of thine enemies. Also the Lord telleth thee that he will make thee an house. And when thy days be fulfilled, and thou shall sleep with thy fathers, I will set up **thy seed** after thee, which shall proceed out of thy bowels, and **I will establish his kingdom. He shall build an house for my name, and I will stablish the throne of his kingdom *for ever.*** I will be his

father, and he shall be my son. If he commit iniquity, I will chasten him with the rod of men, and with the stripes of the children of men: But my mercy shall not depart away from him, as I took it from Saul, whom I put away before thee. And **thine house and thy kingdom** shall be established **for ever** before thee: **thy kingdom** [David's kingdom] **shall be established for ever.** According to all these words, and according to all **this vision,** so did Nathan speak unto **David** [emphasis and commentary mine].

As we examine these Scriptures more closely, let's look again at 2 Samuel 7:10. Here, God tells King David there will come a time "in the future" when His people, Israel, will be appointed **a certain place** and God will plant them **there** and they will dwell in that place and **never *move* again.** Also, no one will be allowed **to afflict them any more as beforetime.**

Anyone knowing the present history of this world and reading his Bible in sincerity surely is persuaded this has not completely happened *yet.*

Also, we notice in this series of Verses that 2 Samuel 7:16 provides us with some new information concerning King David. It simply states: David's house and David's kingdom shall be established **forever before him; also his *throne* shall be established forever.**

I have already mentioned that I recently talked with people who did not know how to define the word *forever,* but I think *Webster's Dictionary* does a tremendous job. We read: **"for eternity, for always, endlessly."**

I feel the reason many people have such a problem with David's promises is because they don't examine 2 Samuel 7:15 with an open mind. We read concerning David's future seed: "But my mercy shall not depart away from him, as I took it from Saul, whom I put away before thee." Also, we find in

Psalm 89:1-4,20-37 a much stronger definitive of God's position on this promise He has made to King David in 2 Samuel 7:15. Let us read these Verses in Psalm Chapter 89 with the definition of "forever" still fresh in our minds:

> I will sing of the mercies of the LORD **for ever:** with my mouth will I make known thy faithfulness to all generations. For I have said, Mercy shall be built up **for ever:** Thy faithfulness shalt thou establish in the heavens. I have made a covenant with my chosen, I have sworn unto **David my servant, Thy *seed* will I establish for ever, and build up *thy throne* to *all* generations. Selah.** . . . I have found David my servant; with my holy oil have I anointed him: With whom my hand shall be established: **Mine arm** also shall strengthen him. The enemy shall not exact upon him; nor the son of wickedness afflict him. And I will beat down his foes before his face, and plague them that hate him. [Wow! How many times has history proven this prophecy to be true?] But my faithfulness and my mercy shall be with him: and in my name shall **his horn [Jesus Christ]** be exalted. I will set his hand also in the sea, and his right hand in the rivers. He shall cry unto me, Thou art my father, my God, and the rock of my salvation. Also I will make him **my firstborn [Jesus Christ], higher than the kings of the earth.** My mercy will I keep for him **for evermore,** and my covenant shall stand fast with him. His **seed [Jesus Christ]** also will I make to endure **for ever,** and *his throne* **as the days of heaven.** If his children forsake my law, and walk not in my judgments; If they break my statutes, and keep not my commandments; Then will I visit their transgression with the rod, and their iniquity with stripes. **Nevertheless, my loving kindness will I not utterly take from him, nor suffer my faithfulness to fail.** My covenant will I not break, nor alter the thing that is

gone out of my lips. Once have I sworn by my holiness that I will not lie to David. His seed shall endure **for ever, and his throne as the sun before me**. **It shall be established for ever as the moon, and as a faithful witness in heaven.** Selah. [Emphasis and all commentary mine.]

As we know, the road to God's final will in our lives is sometimes marked with many hard knocks and disappointments. It is no different in the case of God establishing His Kingdom. The history is long, with many setbacks being suffered by God's people, before and after the cross. However, God has never lost a battle and He never will—Praise His Name!

You see, my friend, God's prophetic Word does not depend upon my actions or your actions, what I believe or what you believe, for fulfillment. God's Word only depends on His sovereignty, His holiness, His ability to bring to pass the things He has purposed in His will, based on what He views in the world below. If my Holy God said it in future prophecy, He has already seen it come to pass. This would make it a done deal as far as God is concerned! Even if God wanted to change His mind about future things, He could not do so because Psalms 138:2b tells us: "**. . . for thou hast magnified thy word above all thy name.**"

It seems as if we could hear our precious Lord and Savior praying to His Heavenly Father now in Matthew 6:9-10: "Our Father which art in heaven, Hallowed be thy name. Thy kingdom come, thy will be done in earth, as it is in heaven."

I believe as times get more and more difficult in these last days, we, as the people of God, will begin to pray this prayer in a more sincere way than we have ever prayed. Soon we will all cry in unison as John did in Revelation 22:20: "**AMEN. Even so, come, Lord Jesus**" [emphasis mine].

If you do not know Jesus Christ as your Lord and Savior,

please don't wait for some alternate plan. The only way into peace in our soul and paradise in **The Last Eden** is the way purchased by our Lord and Savior Jesus Christ on the old rugged cross.

What does the future hold for the bride-elect of our Lord?

Is Heaven only some ethereal fog bank in the sky where everyone is sleeping or strumming on a harp, as some religions teach?

Is there a future time of rule and authority on this planet by God's Son of which all the prophets of God wrote? Also, Jesus Christ demanded it should come before we reach our final destination in Revelation, Chapters 21 and 22. This New Heaven and New Earth (described in these two Chapters) is God's final Eden because here in this new and final paradise, God Himself will have made **all things new!**

The Word of our God has good news for every born-again believer. The King is coming, and I sure am glad I know Him in the free pardon of my sins! What Jesus did on Calvary made all the difference!

But before He arrives on Planet Earth with His newly married wife, there are many more things God has seen accomplished in prophecy. As we endeavor to go **Beyond the Revelation,** it is my desire to bring to light a few more of those things.

In these few pages of Chapter Six, hopefully we have given you ample proof that **the King will be revealed.** He is coming to Planet Earth.

But just in case we have not convinced someone who might still be a little skeptical, consider this:

If Jesus Christ is not coming to Earth, why the fuss concerning the false christ on Earth whom both Daniel and John positively identify? If the Bible tells of a false christ (beast) which will rule the entire planet in false peace, should this not suggest that the **real** Christ, Jesus, will rule this planet in real peace, as He with eyes as a flame of fire comes from Heaven to Earth (Revelation 19:12). If Revelation 19:12 is not talking about Jesus coming to Earth, then we would need to know who will put down the Satan incarnate Antichrist. Will he be allowed to continue on and on, wreaking havoc in the human family forever?

The Holy Bible does not teach such foolishness, but teaches in Revelation 19:19-21 these words of truth. We read:

> And I saw the beast and the kings of the earth, and their armies, gathered together to make war against him [Jesus] that sat on the horse [see Revelation 19:13], and against his army [Saints and Angels: see 2 Thessalonians 1:7-10; Revelation 19:14]. And the beast was taken, and with him the false prophet that wrought miracles before him, with which he deceived them that had received the mark of the beast, and them that worshipped his image. These **both** were cast alive into a lake of fire burning with brimstone. And the remnant [armies] were slain with the sword of him that sat on the horse, which sword proceeded out of his mouth: and all the fowls were filled with **their flesh** [emphasis and commentary mine].

In closing Chapter Six, once again be reminded that God's Saints do not fight at Armageddon; our Savior will (as He did at Calvary) fight alone! Read again Isaiah 63:1-6:

> Who is this that cometh from Edom, with dyed garments from Bozrah? this that is glorious in his apparel, traveling in the greatness of his strength? I that speak in righteousness: mighty to save. [Only Jesus Christ can save.] Wherefore art thou **red in thine apparel,** and thy garments like him

that treadeth in the winefat? I have trodden the winepress ***alone;* and of the people there was none with me:** for I will tread them [the nations] in mine anger, and trample them in my fury; and **their blood shall be sprinkled upon my garments, and I will stain all my raiment.** For the day of vengeance is in my heart, and the year of my redeemed is come. And I looked, and there was **none to help;** and I wondered that there was none to uphold: therefore mine own arm brought salvation unto me; and my fury, it upheld me. And I will tread down the people in mine anger, and make them drunk in my fury, and I will bring down their strength *to the earth* [emphasis and commentary mine].

As we move into Chapter Seven, I will take the Scriptures of Revelation 19:11-21 and *move* **Beyond the Revelation.**

Chapter Seven

Jesus Christ Is Israel's God, After All!

In this Chapter, we have *moved* **Beyond the Revelation of Jesus Christ to Planet Earth.** Let's look in Scripture at some of the glorious Millennium events taking place **after His Revelation to this planet.**

To many people who would pick up a KJV text Bible and begin to read what is written in its holy pages, the Word of God would seem to be a series of genealogical records and events of men and women who lived in the past.

Well, I will readily admit this is true; however, as we have plainly seen in Chapters One through Six of this manuscript, the Bible is much more than a book of genealogy. No genealogy book would have 774,747 words that all agree from front to back!

In reality, the Holy Bible is a God-breathed and God-preserved account of all creation; the fall of man into sin (Genesis 3:1-19); God's plan to redeem fallen man from his sins (Genesis 3:21; John 3:16); also, His plan to redeem all creation (Romans 8:18-23). However, all this redemption is to be accomplished through maintaining a pure seed—from Adam to the human mother of Jesus, the virgin Mary, being the seed of David according to the flesh. As we have noted in this manuscript, Satan did his best to pollute this lineage and stop this God-Man, Messiah, Jesus Christ, from being born of a poor, common, virgin Jewish woman, but he ultimately failed. Though born in a stable, wrapped in swaddling clothes, and laid in a manger, His story is still the world's greatest story. From Genesis to Revelation, Jesus Christ has an eternal, traceable existence and promise (from the first page to the last)! **No man *in history* ever changed history as Jesus did!**

In light of this indisputable fact, **His revelation** at the end of what is commonly called Daniel's seventieth week (Daniel 2:34-35,44-45; 7:18,27; 9:24), with **all** His Saints (1 Thessalonians 3:13; Jude 14-15), is of the utmost importance to the Adam race (but especially to the Jewish people). I will comment more on this subject, later.

In Chapter Seven, we will look one final time in Revelation 19:7-8, 11-21 and witness **Heaven being opened,** revealing Jesus Christ (and His newly-married wife) *moving* in power and great glory to Planet Earth. We read Revelation 19:7-8: "Let us be glad and rejoice, and give honour to him: **for the marriage of the Lamb *is come*, and his wife hath made herself ready. And to *her* was granted that *she* should be arrayed in fine linen, clean and white: for the fine linen is the righteousness of *saints*."**

In the realm of religion, we have two categories of people. Down in the backwoods of Middle Tennessee, we commonly refer to these as **Saints** or **ain'ts.** One of my blessed preacher brothers once put it this way: Either you is or you ain't— a Saint. In Revelation 19:7-8 "her" and "she" has to do with Saints, not ain'ts.

It is imperative we remember: If Jesus Christ was not revealed to this planet, most of the prophecies of the Old and New Testaments concerning Saints would not be fulfilled! See Jude: 14-15; 1 Thessalonians 2:19; 3:13; 5:23; Zechariah 14:5b; Psalm 149:1-9; Isaiah 35:10, etc.).

As we watch Jesus ride out of Heaven on His white horse, we must not forget, once, that we (the espoused bride of Jesus Christ) are called **up** to meet the Lord in the air at the Rapture. We will forever be with the Lord. If the Lord is in Heaven, His Church is in Heaven. If the Lord comes to Earth, His Church comes to Earth. If the Lord *moves* to the New Heaven and the New Earth, His Church will *move* with Him. Glory!!!

Let me insert, as we are making all these *moves,* Jesus Christ will not be our co-pilot. If the Lord is not **in you and you in the Lord** (John 15:4-7), you are not **in** this number! The Holy Ghost never rides in the passenger seat; He rides *in you.* **It would do all religious people well to make sure He is living in their soul! You can baptize a person until they know every crawfish, tadpole, and minnow in the creek on a first name basis, but if that person dosen't have Jesus in their soul, they will die in their sins! Jesus said: "You must be born again or you will in no wise see or enter the kingdom of God."**

Listen as our God takes His Son **Beyond the Revelation** in Revelation 19:11-21:

> And I saw **heaven opened,** and behold a white horse; and he that sat upon him was called Faithful and True, and in righteousness he doth judge and make war. His eyes were as a flame of fire, and on **his** head were many crowns; and he had a name written, that no man knew, but he himself. And he was clothed with a vesture dipped in blood: and **his name is called The Word of God.** And the armies which **were in heaven** followed him upon white horses, **clothed in fine linen, white and clean.** [Read again 1 Thessalonians 1:10; 3:13; Jude 14-15.] And **out of his mouth goeth a sharp sword,** that with it he should smite the nations [read Isaiah 11:4b]: and **he shall rule them** [the nations]

with a rod of iron: and he treadeth the winepress of the fierceness and wrath of Almighty God. And he hath on his vesture and on his thigh a name written, **KING OF KINGS, AND LORD OF LORDS.** And I saw an angel standing in the sun; and he cried with a loud voice, saying to **all the fowls** that fly in the midst of heaven, Come and gather yourselves together to the supper of the great God; That ye may eat the flesh of kings, and the flesh of captains, and the flesh of mighty men, and the flesh of horses, and of them that sit on them, and the flesh of **all men,** both free and bond, both small and great. [Wow, what an unusual meal!] And **I saw the beast, and the kings of the earth, and their armies, gathered together to make war against him that sat on the horse, and against his army.** And the **beast** was taken, and with him the **false prophet** that wrought miracles before him, with which he deceived them that had received the mark of the beast, and them that worshipped his image. These **both** were cast **alive** into a lake of fire burning with brimstone. [The first two occupants of this black, hot lake of fire.] And the remnant [armies of the beast] were slain **with the sword of him that sat upon the horse, which sword proceeded out of his mouth: and all the fowls were filled with their flesh** [emphasis and commentary mine].

As we have, previously noted, the **Revelation of Jesus Christ** is not just my only hope, not just your only hope, not just the only hope for the Nation of Israel, not just the only hope for lost humanity (if they will repent and come to Christ). It is also the only hope for this planet, because all nature will be regenerated in the *day* when Jesus comes **Beyond the Revelation** to reign supreme!

Let's read again of this regeneration (after Christ is revealed to Planet Earth) in Romans 8:18-23:

For I reckon that the sufferings of this present time are not worthy to be compared with **the glory which shall be revealed in *us*** [*us,* being the Lord's true Saints]. For the earnest expectation of the **creature waiteth** for the manifestation of the Sons of God. For **the creature** was made subject to vanity, not willingly, but by reason of him who hath subjected the same in hope. Because **the creature itself also shall be delivered from the bondage of corruption into the glorious liberty of the children of God.** For we know that the **whole creation** groaneth and travileth in pain together until now. And not only they, but ourselves also, which have the first fruits of the Spirit, even we ourselves groan within ourselves, **waiting for the adoption, to wit, the redemption of our body** [emphasis mine].

As we look farther into these Verses, it is interesting to note that the word for **"creature"** and the word for **"creation"** are the very same word in the Greek dictionary. This Greek word is ***ktis-is***, which means **"original formation."** This would cause Romans 8:21 to literally read, "Because the 'original formation' itself, also, shall be delivered from the bondage of corruption into the glorious liberty of the children of God."

In like manner, the *Old Webster's Dictionary* confirms the Greek ***ktis-is*** with these definitions:

» **Creature:** That which is created; Every being, besides the Creator; (The original formation).
» **Creation:** The **act** of creating; (The original formation).

As God kept His promise to physically restore the Nation of Israel, He will also keep His promise to redeem and regenerate all of the creation, **After His Revelation.**

I would think anyone who is aware of the Nation of Israel's history would also be aware of the miracle of God keeping His promises in mankind's history. Israel lay desolate for almost two thousand years. Then, in 1899, a movement began in Europe resulting to Isaiah 66:8 being fulfilled to the letter, and the Nation of Israel being reborn on May 14, 1948!

We read Isaiah 66:8: "Who hath heard such a thing? Who hath seen such things? Shall the earth be made to bring forth **in one day? or shall a *nation* be born at once?** For, as soon as Zion travailed, **she brought forth her children**" [emphasis mine].

This nation truly was born in one day (in the United Nations), just as the prophet had prophesied 2,640 years[28] earlier. However, this prophet did not mention the United Nations. There was no need. He only needed to tell what God (the Holy Spirit) told him to tell concerning this prophecy and rebirth.

If there was no other event in world history to prove the validity of Bible prophecy and the truth of God's Word as a whole, the physical rebirth of the Nation of Israel would do it nicely! Outside the physical birth of God in human flesh through the virgin Mary (David's seed), the physical rebirth of the Nation of Israel just may be the greatest miracle in the last two millennia!

Just as our Holy God used the virgin birth of His Holy Son to propel us into the Grace Dispensation and bring us most of the events recorded in the New Testament on building and maintaining the New Testament church (which will not be dealt with in this manuscript), I believe He is using the physical rebirth of the Nation of Israel to, ultimately, bring about the fulfillment of written prophecy in these last days.

Note: It is my sincere desire, that those who decry and defame the validity of this present reborn nation would take a serious look at some of the Holy Scriptures which

---

28. Ussher, *Annals of the World*

proclaim its rebirth and future glory: Jeremiah 3:14-18; 23:3-8; 31:8-12,35-36; 33:19-26; 46:28; Ezekiel 34:20-31; 36:24-28,33-36; 37:21-25; 39:25-29; Isaiah 11:12; 14:1-2; Acts 1:6-7; Romans 11:25-27, etc. Then they should get on their knees and ask God and then their fellowman for forgiveness.

As we continue to look **Beyond This Revealing of Jesus Christ,** I hope we would note the issue of *why* Jesus Christ has come back to Planet Earth. One reason is to destroy them which destroy the Earth (Revelation 11:18); another is to deal with those nations mistreating the tiny Nation of Israel after its rebirth in May 1948! We read Joel 3:1-2,12:

> For, behold, in those days, and in that time, *when* **I shall bring again the captivity of Judah and Jerusalem,** I [God] will also gather all nations, and will bring them down into the valley of Jehoshaphat [place where Yahweh judgeth[29]] and will plead with them there **for my people and for my Heritage Israel, whom they have scattered among the nations, and parted** *my land* [Whose land? God's land.].
> ... Let the heathen be wakened, and come up to the valley of Jehoshaphat: for there will I sit to judge **all** the heathen round about [emphasis and commentary mine].

In *Strong's Concordance of the Hebrew Language,* we find the word "heritage" defined: "Ref. 5159; *nakh-al-aw*: Something inherited; an heirloom; an estate; a possession." Also, notice in Joel 3:2 that the conjunction "and" between "my people" and "my heritage, Israel." This assures us that two peoples are involved as we *move* beyond the revealing of Jesus Christ to Planet Earth.

It is my opinion these two peoples are the **New Testament**

---
29. Butler, Trent C. *Holman Bible Dictionary*

Church and **the Nation of Israel.**

Now, let's look farther at this judgment issue.

It seems Matthew 25:31-34 picks up this judgment (when Jesus Christ is revealed), as Matthew records these Words of God:

> **When** [not if] the Son of Man **shall *come* in his glory,** and **all** the holy angels with him, **then** shall he sit upon the throne of his glory [David's throne]: And before him shall be gathered **all nations:** and he shall separate **them** one from another, as a shepherd divided his Sheep from the goats: And he [Son of Man] shall set the sheep on his right hand, but the goats on the left. **Then shall the king say unto them on his right hand,** Come ye blessed of my Father, **inherit the *kingdom*** prepared for you from the foundation of the world [emphasis and commentary mine].

If we read the remainder of this Chapter, we will find that Jesus judges sheep and goats strictly on the manner in which they had treated His (Jesus') brethren. We should also note: This judgment is after the **Revealing of Jesus** to the Earth.

Consider these seven things as we look at this judgment in Matthew Chapter 25:

1. There are **no books opened.**
2. There is **no resurrection mentioned.**
3. All persons judged are *living* **nations.**
4. There are *three* classes of these *living* peoples present.
5. They are: **sheep, goats, and brethren.**
6. **All nations *on Earth*** are being judged.
7. Jesus is judging on His throne **after His return to Earth.**

Keeping in context, I would assume Jesus' brethren are a remnant nation of brethren. Jesus is a Jew. The Nation of Israel (at this time) is a remnant nation of Jews, because two-thirds of them will have been killed by the Antichrist as recorded in Zechariah 13:8-9. Would this make Jesus' brethren the Nation of Israel? Well, I would think so! Wouldn't you?

What are your feelings on this Nation of Israel as you evaluate today's conflicting world? Do you love tiny Israel, or do you write them off as you would a bad debt? Are you among the masses that believe that the New Testament Church has replaced Israel as far as God's favor is concerned?

I fear many good, well-meaning Christians are misinformed on the events of prophecy concerning this reborn nation. This could (depending on the attitude of their heart) place them in danger of God's judgment on their life in these last days.

Also, from a national standpoint, America should beware! Our efforts to forcefeed Israel a "land-for-peace" diet has possibly cost us **untold billions in national disasters.** One would only need to check the records to see that each time we broker a land-for-peace deal between Israel and her sworn enemies, we, the American people, suffer miserably! It is my opinion that if this carnage does not stop, we in America may soon lose our sovereignty. No nation in history has survived when they fought against the will of God for Israel. Just a simple look at present events and past history will confirm this fact.

As we *move,* farther, **Beyond the Revelation,** we will read Joel 3:16-21:

> The **Lord** also shall roar out of Zion, and **utter his voice from Jerusalem;** and the heavens and the earth shall shake: but the LORD will be the hope of **his people,** *and* the strength of the **children of Israel** [notice again: two peoples]. **[Note: Jesus coming with His church to defend the Nation of Israel = Armageddon. Armageddon = the end of the con-**

troversy of Zion!!! Read Isaiah 34:1-8.] So shall ye know that I am the LORD your God **dwelling** [living] in Zion, *my* holy mountain: then shall **Jerusalem** be holy, and there shall no stranger pass through her any more. [Read Isaiah Chapters 65-66.] And it shall come to pass in that day, that the mountains shall drop down new wine, and the hills shall flow with milk, and *all* the rivers of **Judah shall flow with *waters,* and a fountain shall come forth of the house of the LORD, and shall water the valley of Shittim.** [There will be more on this fountain and valley later.] Egypt shall be a desolation, and Edom shall be a desolate wilderness, **for the violence against the children of Judah,** because they have shed innocent blood in **their land** [Judah's land]. But **Judah** shall dwell **for ever,** and **Jerusalem** from generation to generation. **For I will cleanse their blood that I have not cleansed: For the LORD dwelleth** [is living] ***in*** **Zion.** [Sounds like a conversion to Jesus Christ to me!] [emphasis and all commentary mine].

These Verses from Joel do not leave *even the most hardened skeptic* any place to hide. Jesus Christ has *moved* **Beyond His Revelation** and is at this time working full force in the Millennium.

As we continue to read these Scriptures concerning the Nation of Israel, please, consider this:

1. If there was no **Nation of Israel,** there would be no Battle of Armageddon for Christ to fight (alone)! (Revelation 16:14-16; 19:11-21; Isaiah 63:1-6)
2. If there was no **Nation of Israel,** there could be nothing to prompt Antichrist to bring all nations against Jerusalem at Armeggedon! (Zechariah 12:1-9)
3. If there was no **Nation of Israel,** there would be no one for the Antichrist to attack and destroy two parts (two-

thirds), leaving one part (one- third) to be preserved by God's supernatural protection! (Zechariah 13:8-9; Romans 11:25-27)

4. If there was no **Nation of Israel,** after two-thirds are destroyed in Zechariah 13:9b, Israel could not flee to the valley of the mountains that reaches unto Azal. (Zechariah 14:5a)
5. If there was no **Nation of Israel,** Jerusalem would not be trodden down of the Gentiles, until the times of the Gentiles be fulfilled (Luke 21:24). Note: A Gentile is someone who is not a Jew. Israel is a Jewish state. Jerusalem is a Jewish city. Jesus is a (God incarnate) Jew!
6. If there was no **Nation of Israel,** for whom will the Antichrist build a temple on Mt. Moriah, as foretold during the seventieth week of Daniel's prophecy? (Daniel 9:27; 12:11; Matt. 24:15-16)
7. If there was no **Nation of Israel,** who are the twelve tribes whom the angel sealed in Revelation 7:1-8?
8. If there was no **Nation of Israel,** why do their tribal names appear on the twelve gates of the holy New Jerusalem in the new Earth? (Revelation 21:12)

As you can see, the list would exhaust many more pages of this work if we attempted to write all the things mentioned in Scripture concerning the re-establishing of this tiny Nation of Israel in these last days.

Oh, yes! This valley of the mountains mentioned in Zechariah 14:5a, and other places, just happens to be the very place Jesus Christ will come (with *all* of His Saints 14:5b) to deliver the remnant of Israel after they have fled from the Antichrist in the last half of Daniel's seventieth week. But, before Jesus goes to the valley, it is at least a possibility that He will return to the Mount of Olives, as He said in Acts 1:11.

In Zechariah 14:4, we read: "And his [Jesus] feet shall stand in that day upon the Mount of Olives, which is before Jerusalem on the east, and the Mount of Olives shall cleave [split open] in the midst thereof toward the east and toward the west, and there shall be a very great valley; and half of the mountain will remove toward the **north** and half of it toward the **south**" [emphasis and commentary mine].

I have personally stood on the Mount of Olives more than fourteen times. I have not seen one crack, *YET!* But, just now, I said to myself: *Be patient, for it will happen some day!* Our God is longsuffering; God's Word has never failed. Remember how long God waited on man to repent in the days of Noah!

Also, as I mentioned, in the Book of Acts we read the account of how Jesus "left" for Heaven. We read Acts 1:10-12:

> And while they looked stedfastly toward heaven as he went up, behold, two men stood by them in white apparel; Which also said, Ye men of Galilee, why stand ye gazing up into heaven? **this same Jesus,** which is taken up from you into heaven, **shall so come in like manner as ye have seen him go into heaven.** Then returned they unto Jerusalem from the **mount called Olivet,** which is from Jerusalem a sabbath day's journey [emphasis mine].

The Book of Ezekiel gives specific detail of **why** this mountain splits at **the Revelation of Jesus Christ to begin His reign.** We read Ezekiel 47:1,7-12:

> Afterward he brought me again unto the door of the house; and, behold, **waters** issued out from under the threshold of the house eastward: for the forefront of the house stood toward the east, and the **waters** came down from under the right side of the house, at the south side of the **alter.** . . . Now when I had returned, behold, at the **bank of the riv-**

er were very many trees on the one side and on the other. Then said he unto me, These **waters** issue out toward the **east country,** and go down into the desert, **and go into the sea: Which being brought forth into the sea,** [Dead Sea] **These waters shall be healed.** And it shall come to pass, that every thing that liveth, which moveth, whithersoever the **rivers** shall come, shall live: and there shall be a very great multitude of fish, because **these waters** shall come thither: for **they shall be healed; and everything shall live whether the river cometh.** And it shall come to pass, that the **fishers** shall stand upon it from **En-gedi** even unto **En-eglaim;** they shall be a place to spread forth nets; their fish shall be according to their kinds, **as** the fish of the great sea [Mediterranean Sea], exceeding many. But the miry places thereof and the marishes thereof shall not be healed; they shall be given to salt. And by the river upon the bank thereof, on this side and on that side, **shall grow all trees for meat, whose leaf shall not fade, neither shall the fruit thereof be consumed: it shall bring forth new fruit according to his months, because their waters they issued out of the sanctuary: and the fruit thereof shall be for meat, and the leaf thereof for medicine** [emphasis and commentary mine].

Bless the HOLY name of Jesus. He, truly, is God incarnate!

Wow, what a river! Joel 3:18 and, more specifically, Ezekiel 47:1 have already told us this river coming from under the threshold of the house of the LORD and running through the Mount of Olives shall water the valley of Shittim. Where is Shittim? Our Bible dictionary[30] identifies Shittim as a large area in Moab (modern-day Jordan), directly across the Jordan

---

30. Butler, *Holman Bible Dictionary*

River from Jericho and northeast of the Dead Sea. Those who have toured this area would be familiar with this definition.

Zechariah 14:8 speaks giving us new information about this river. We read: "And it shall be in that day that **living waters** [plural] shall go out from Jerusalem; **half of them** toward the **former sea,** and **half of them** toward the **hinder sea:** in summer and in winter shall it be" (emphasis and commentary mine).

Since Ezekiel 47:1-12 speaks of **rivers** (plural), and Zechariah 14:8 speaks of **rivers** (plural), I think we should look for another river. Don't you? We find it in the present Scripture of Zechariah 14:8. It is encoded in the wording: Half of *them* toward the **former** sea and half of *them* toward the **hinder** sea. **River running east; river running west. Amen!**

There are two seas in the land of Israel: "the Med" and "the Dead," or the Mediterranean Sea and the Dead Sea.

Ezekiel 47:9a has told us: "And it shall come to pass, that everything that liveth, which moveth, **withersoever the *rivers* shall come shall *live.*"** Would this not make both these rivers "living waters"? I would think so. Wouldn't you?

Knowing this has become reality, when we have *moved* **Beyond the Revelation** into the glorious Millennium, I think we should consider what God is doing from a worldwide scenario. Let's see what this **river** flowing to the **west** (toward the Mediterranean) will involve. A simple examination of God's Earth on a globe or map will tell the story.

All waters of Planet Earth will be healed (Zechariah 14:8; Ezekiel 47:9) because all waters connect, with the exception of the Dead Sea which has no outlet, and the rivers flowing to the former and hinder seas (Zechariah14:8) will take care of that! One river to the Mediterranean Sea, one river to the Dead Sea. No matter how much the topography of the planet changes, our Holy God knows His business!

Notice, that the rivers get their water from rain. The clouds get their rain from the seas. The rivers, then, send their water back to the seas. In this glorious Millennial day (with the devil bound—Revelation 20:1-3) there will be worldwide healing through these **living waters!**

(Read Ezekiel 7:8-9; Romans 8:21; Isaiah 14:7-8; 51:3).

Those who study prophecy know Revelation Chapter 16 records a cataclysmic shaking of the Earth in the end of Daniel's seventieth week. This caused me to wonder how the face of this planet will look after these judgments in the Book of Revelation come to pass. One thing we can know for sure: the Bible says these **rivers flow east and west** and Zechariah 14:10 tell us Jerusalem will be lifted *up* in that day. More on this high place, later.

Psalm Chapter 46 breaks in on this river subject with the good news:

> GOD is our refuge and strength, a very present help in trouble. Therefore will not we fear, though the earth be removed, **and though the mountains be carried into the midst of the sea** [see Revelation16:20); Though the waters thereof roar and be troubled, though the mountains shake with the swelling thereof. Selah. **There is a *river*, the streams** [plural] **whereof shall make glad the *city of God*, the holy place of the tabernacles of the Most High. God is in the midst of her** [the city, Jerusalem]; she shall not be moved: God shall help her, and that right early. The heathen **raged, the kingdoms were moved:** he uttered his voice, the earth **melted. The Lord of hosts is with *us*;** the God of Jacob is our refuge. Selah. Come, behold the works of the Lord, **what desolations he hath made in the earth** [Great Tribulation—Revelation 16-18]. **He maketh *wars to cease unto the end of the earth;*** he breaketh the bow, and cutteth the

spear in sunder; he burneth the chariot in the fire. [Read Isaiah 2:1-4.] Be still and know that I am God: I will be exalted among the heathen, **I will be exalted *in the earth.*** [Read Zechariah 14:9-11.] **The LORD of hosts is with us;** the God of Jacob is our refuge. Selah [emphasis and commentary mine].

I sincerely hope we *all* have noticed in these Verses where our Lord Jesus Christ has located Himself. It is with **"us"** (V. 11) on **"Earth"** (V. 9).

I know this sounds too good to be true. However, the reality is that Jesus Christ has *moved* "**Beyond the Revelation**" to Jerusalem, His city (Matthew 5:35), right smack-dab in the middle of Planet Earth! Thus, His desire is fulfilled which began with Joseph gathering wealth in Egypt! God will finally have His house on this present Planet Earth and will live with His people for one thousand glorious years! This will give the Earth its much-deserved Sabbath rest. Holy is His Name!

Moving farther **Beyond the Revelation**, we must not leave out the great prophet **Jeremiah** as he speaks of these *rivers* in this day of glory for Jesus Christ, His wife the church, Israel, His heritage, and the whole creation Planet Earth. We read in Jeremiah 31:7-12:

> For thus saith the LORD; Sing with gladness **for Jacob,** and shout among the chief of the nations: publish ye, praise ye, and say, **O LORD, save thy people, *the remnant of Israel.*** Behold I will bring **them** from the north country, and gather **them** from the coasts of the earth, and with **them** the blind and the lame, the woman with child and her that travaileth with child together: **a great company shall return thither.** [Return where? To the place where the rivers are coming from under the throne of God's House at Jerusalem—Eze-

kiel 47:1]. They shall come with weeping, and with supplications will I lead them: **I will cause them to walk by the rivers of waters in a straight way,** wherein they shall not stumble; for I am a father to Israel, and Ephraim is my firstborn. Hear the word of the LORD, O ye nations, and declare it in the isles afar off, and say, **He that scattered Israel will gather him, and keep him, as a shepherd doth his flock.** For the LORD hath [past tense] redeemed **Jacob,** and ransomed him from the hand of him [Gentile nations] that was stronger than he. Therefore they shall come and sing in the **height of Zion,** and shall flow together in the goodness of the LORD, for wheat, and for wine, and for oil, and for the young of the flock and of the herd: And their soul shall be as a watered garden; **and they** [Israel] **shall not sorrow any more at all** [emphasis and commentary mine].

Folks, if we are saved, these Verses should light a fire in our souls. Any "professing" Saint of God who is against Jesus Christ redeeming the Nation of Israel (or anyone else who is lost) is either deceived or riding in an elevator that does not go *up!*

Looking farther, as we would expect from our great God, He gives **Isaiah the prophet** this prophecy concerning opening these *rivers* **in high places** and what will be the result of their opening in that day. Read very carefully Isaiah 41:14–20.

Fear not, thou worm **Jacob,** and ye men of **Israel;** I will help thee, saith the LORD, and thy redeemer, the Holy One of Israel. **Behold, I will make *thee* a new sharp threshing instrument having teeth: *thou* shalt thresh the mountains, and beat them small, and shalt make the hills as chaff. *Thou* shalt fan them, and the wind shall carry them away, and the whirlwind shall scatter them: and *thou* shalt rejoice in the** LORD, **and shalt glory in the**

Holy One of Israel [Jesus Christ]. When the poor and needy seek water, and there is none, and their tongue faileth for thirst, I the LORD will hear them, I the **God of Israel** will not forsake them. **I will open *rivers* [plural] in high places, and fountains [plural] in the midst of the valleys: I will make the wilderness a pool of water, and the dry land springs of water.** I will plant in the wilderness the cedar, the shittah tree; and the myrtle, and the oil tree; and the pine and the box tree together: That they [the nations] may see and know, and consider, and understand together, that the hand of the LORD hath done this, and the **Holy One of Israel** hath created it [emphasis and commentary mine].

I think a good question concerning Isaiah 41:15-16 would be: How can the wind carry away hills and mountains? Is there a possibility this new, sharp threshing instrument mentioned in these two Verses could be some form of nuclear destruction? I suppose only time will tell, but remember that this worm, Jacob, has *promised help* coming from the Holy One of Israel during his time of trouble. This Holy One of Israel just happens to be a carpenter from Nazareth who was born God incarnate through a virgin named Mary, after she was impregnated by God, the Holy Ghost. This God incarnate grew to adulthood and willingly gave His life on a cruel Roman cross as an acceptable substitute for *all* lost sinners who will come to Him on gospel terms. He was laid in a rich man's tomb and three days later got up and walked out on death. Forty days later, from a hill just east of Jerusalem, He ascended back to His Father's right hand in the third Heaven. Since no man or angel in this universe can prove He is not still there, I expect He has kept His Word He gave in John Chapter 14.

It is my opinion that this God incarnate will soon Rapture His espoused bride *up* to that same third Heaven, as we are symbolized in the twenty-four elders which were seated surrounding the throne of God. It is also my opinion that we find this event prophesied in Revelation 3:21, fulfilled in Revelation 4:1-4, and confirmed in Revelation 5:8-10.

Notice: After the Rapture event, the espoused bride in Heaven will:

1. Appear at the Judgment Seat of Christ where **crowns** are given (2 Corinthians 5:10; Revelation 4:4).
2. See the **four beasts** in God's throne (Revelation 4:6).
3. View (what I believe is the title deed to Planet Earth—the seven-sealed scroll) handed to Christ, and subsequent **coronation of the Lamb as King** (Revelation 5:1-10).
4. Stand in awe as the **sealing of the 144,000 Jews** (twelve thousand from each tribe) takes place (Revelation 7:1-8).
5. Rejoice with the **great multitude** of martyred saints as they come *up* **out of great tribulation** to Heaven (Revelation 7:9-17).
6. Stand in silence, about the space of half an hour, as the **seven trumpets** are about to be sounded (Revelation 8:1).
7. Wonder with the angels as God seals what the **seven thunders** uttered (Revelation 10:1-4).
8. Watch with amazement as the **two witnesses** prophesy 1,260 days, forty-two months, three and one-half years, or time, times, and half a time, down on Planet Earth (Revelation 11:2-3; 12:14; Daniel 12:7).
9. Rejoice, with **the Woman, Israel,** as she is given two wings of a great eagle, taking her to her place of protection in the wilderness as she awaits her deliverance at Armageddon (Revelation 12:14; Zechariah 14:5).
10. Observe the **beast out of the sea** and the **beast out of the Earth** as they work their evil doings (Revelation 17:1-18).
11. Marvel and rejoice over another woman, **the great whore,**

as she is given her just rewards for the atrocities committed to the human family (Revelation 18; 19:2).
12. Hear the voice from God's throne say: "**The marriage supper of the Lamb** *is come*" (Revelation 19:4–10).
13. Watch as Jesus Christ mounts His white horse for that triumphant ride toward Armageddon (Revelation 19:11). (No colt to be ridden in this day!)
14. **Follow** Jesus on our white horses, wearing our white fine linen granted to saints at the marriage of the Lamb in Revelation 19:8 (Revelation 19:14). Note: Some have suggested this married wife of Jesus Christ (clothed in white) looked like clouds when the Apostle John saw his vision in Revelation 1:7. We read again: "Behold, he cometh *with* **clouds;** and *every* eye shall see him, and they also which pierced him; and all kindred's of the earth shall wail because of him. Even so, Amen." Since Verse 7 is speaking of His Revelation and not the Rapture, it certainly sounds possible to me.
15. View this **threshing of the hills and mountains** (Isaiah 41:15).
16. Rejoice with all creation as **Satan, the red dragon,** is bound in the bottomless pit for a thousand years (Revelation 12:3–4; 20:1–3).
17. Possibly be gathered by the angels from the four winds of Heaven where we have watched and waited as Jesus takes care of delivering Israel at Armageddon (Matthew 24:30–31; Mark 13:26–27).

With these events digested, let's read again Joel 3:9–21:

Proclaim ye this among the Gentiles; Prepare war, wake up the mighty men, let all the men of war draw near; let them come up: Beat your plowshares into swords, and your pruning hooks into spears: let the weak say, I am strong. Assemble yourselves, and come, all ye heathen, and gather yourselves together round about: thither cause thy mighty ones to **come down,** O LORD. Let the heathen be wakened, and come up to the valley of Jesoshaphat: for there will I sit **to judge** all the heathen round about. Put ye in the sickle, for the harvest is ripe: come, get you down; for the press is full, the fats overflow; for their wickedness is great. Multitudes, multitudes, in the valley of decision: for the day of the LORD is near in the valley of decision. The sun and the moon shall be darkened, and the stars shall withdraw their shining. The LORD also shall roar out of Zion, and **utter his voice from Jerusalem;** and the heavens and the earth shall shake: but the LORD will be the hope of **his people** [New Testament Church], and the strength of the **children of Israel** [emphasis and commentary mine].

Then, after the Revelation and Battle of Armageddon:

So shall ye know that **I am the LORD your God dwelling** [living] **in Zion, my holy mountain: then shall Jerusalem be holy, and there shall no strangers pass through her any more.** [Praise God!!!] And it shall come to pass in that day, that the mountains shall drop down new wine, and the hills shall flow with milk, **and all the *rivers of Judah shall flow with waters,* and a fountain shall come forth of the house of the LORD, and shall water the valley of Shittim.** Egypt shall be a desolation, and Edom shall be a desolate wilderness, for the violence against the children of Judah, **because they have shed innocent blood in their land.** But, **Judah shall dwell forever, and Jerusalem from generation to generation.** For I will cleanse their blood [Israel's blood—Romans 11:25-27] that I have not cleansed; **for** the LORD dwelleth [is living] **in Zion** [emphasis and commentary mine].

However, we must not forget: Christ *moving* **Beyond the Revelation** will not culminate until the end of the Millennium where we will view 1 Corinthians 15:24–27 in its fulfillment. We read:

> Then cometh the end, when he shall have delivered *up* the kingdom to God, even the Father; **when he shall have put down all rule and all authority and power.** For **he must reign, till he hath put all enemies under his feet.** The last enemy that shall be destroyed is **death.** [This happens at the end of the millennium—Revelation 20:14.] For **he hath put all things under his feet,** But **when** he saith all things are put under him, it is manifest that he is excepted, which did put all things under him.

After this is accomplished, all true Saints will be brought into the New Heaven and the New Earth, wherein dwelleth righteousness!

Now, let's *move* to Chapter Eight where God and His people **begin *anew*** in the New Earth, which (according to the Scriptures) I believe to be the **Last Eden!**

Just as God used **eight people** to repopulate the Earth (purged by water) in Noah's day, also, **eight being the number of new beginnings**[31] and **Eight being the number of the next Chapter,** I feel we should be able to locate **"eight"** in reference to **The Last Eden.** Take a look at the **"eighth seven"** in Epilogue (at the end of this manuscript) and see if you agree.

---

31. Hutchings, *Master Mathematician*

Chapter Eight

New Beginnings

With the Millennium being past, and the devil that deceived the nations (after he was loosed from his thousand-year prison term in the bottomless pit) being thrown into the lake of fire; with the present Heaven and Earth having been dissolved with consuming fire, and the White Throne Judgment coming to completion (read Revelation 20:7–15; 21:1; 2 Peter 3:1–13), we will now hear from Dr. Henry Morris[32] on 2 Peter 3:10–12. Dr. Morris was a tremendous person whom I admired greatly. He writes:

> The day of the lord will be terminated (at the end of the Millennium) with the long-awaited renovation of the old earth by fire. The earth will not be annihilated any more than the old earth was annihilated at the time of the flood, but will be completely changed and purified (made new) as it were. All the elements themselves have been under God's curse (Gen. 3:17–19); so they must be "burned up" along with the vast evidences of decay and death, now, preserved as fossils in the earth's crust. Possibly this will be a global atomic fission reaction (note the word "dissolved" in 2 Peter 3:11), or else

---

32. Wilmington, H. L. *Eschatology 101*

simply a vast explosive disintegration involving transformation of the chemical energy of the elements into heat, light and sound energy. What remains after the global fiery disintegration will be other forms of energy, so that, although God's principle of conservation still holds; the solid earth will seem to have fled away (Revelation 20:11).

In my forty-two-plus years of study in the prophetic Word, I have always contended this Earth (when destroyed) will definitely change from solid to vapor, because of the Scriptural wording in Revelation 20:11 and 21:1. However, I could not come to grips with such Scriptures as Psalm 104:5; 78:69; and Ecclesiastes 1:4, which teach the Earth will abide forever. Dr Morris has helped me with some excellent points in **his view** of the consummation of this present Heaven and Earth, which I feel are pertinent to this Chapter.

With the realization that the blessed Holy Scriptures teach in Psalm 37:11 and Matthew 5:5 that the **meek shall inherit the Earth**, I am thinking that God's Saints should certainly look for another Earth and Heaven to inherit after this one is burned, by whatever method God uses! After all, none of us know exactly how God will melt the elements; we just know He will. See again 2 Peter 3:10-13.

Well, we are not disappointed. In Revelation 21:1, John writes: "And I saw a new heaven and a new earth: for the first heaven and the first earth **were passed away; and there was no more sea."**

In this Chapter, we will now *move* from the first Heaven, first Earth and first Jerusalem **into** the New Heaven, New Earth, and holy New Jerusalem. There will be more on this holy Jerusalem later.

I would like to say: It will surely feel good to be in a land where God is always with His people in this holy place... **forever!** The evidence presented in this manuscript gives many proofs this has been His desire from the beginning of creation.

All tears have been wiped away in this land.

No one can die, because death and hell no longer exist in this land. The devil and all—whether angel or human—who chose to follow Satan, are in the lake of fire, where they will die the second death... forever.

No one can be sorrowful, sick, or have pain in this land, because this type of misery passed away with the first Heaven and the first Earth. I know it is hard to believe, but your athlete's foot fungus will not be present in this land! Headaches and heartaches are all gone in this land! Arthr and all his "itis" brothers (bursitis, tendonitis, sinusitis, etc.) will not be present in this land.

There will be no need to argue with our fellow Saints, because all things will be perfectly known in this land. We certainly can't comprehend it now; but God will be faithful to make **all things new** in this land—"made" only for the meek. Really! (See Matthew 5:5).

I would think we all could conclude that we who have arrived in this land have arrived in God's final Eden!

We wrote a good bit about **wealth** in Chapter Five and told how our God (through mankind) gathered this wealth to accomplish His will in building Himself a house on this present Earth, in which He might dwell with **His people, Israel.**

Here in the New Heaven, New Earth, and holy New Jerusalem, Jesus Christ has again used "gold" to build both He and His wife not just a house, but a city with dwelling places inside!

After the Lord had risen from the dead, He promised His Saints He was going to His Father's house to prepare a **"place"** for them (in the third Heaven). (Read John 14:1–3.) The following Scriptures define this **"place"** as New Jerusalem.

NOTE: Some have suggested in the past that this holy New Jerusalem is only a symbolic picture of the New Testament Church, and should never be viewed as a literal city. I would only reply: "Listen very carefully as we read these descriptive Scriptures from Revelation 21:9-27.

And there came unto me one of the seven angels which had the seven vials full of the seven last plagues, and talked with me, saying, Come hither, **I will shew thee the bride, the Lamb's wife.** And he carried me away in the spirit to a great and high mountain, **and shewed me that great city, the holy Jerusalem, descending out of heaven from God,** Having the glory of God: and her light was like unto a stone most precious, even like a jasper stone, clear as crystal: And had a wall great and high, and had **twelve gates,** and at the gates **twelve angels,** and names written thereon, which are the **names of the twelve tribes of the children of Israel:** On the **east** three gates; on the **north** three gates; on the **south** three gates; and on the **west** three gates. And the wall of the city had **twelve foundations,** and in them the **names of the twelve apostles of the Lamb.** And he that talked with me had a golden reed to measure the city, and the gates thereof, and the wall thereof. And **the city lieth foursquare,** and the length is as large as the breadth: and he measured the city with the reed, **twelve thousand furlongs. The length and the breadth and the height of it are equal.** And he measured the wall thereof, an **hundred and forty and four-cubits,** according to the measure of a man, that is, of the angel. And the building of the wall of it was of **jasper: and the city was pure gold, like unto clear glass.** And the foundations of the wall of the city were garnished with all manner of precious stones. The first foundation was **jasper;** the second, **sapphire;** the third, a **chalcedony;** the fourth, an **emerald;** The fifth, **sardonyx;** the sixth, **sardius;** the seventh, **chrysolite;** the eighth, **beryl;** the ninth, a **topaz;** the tenth, a **chrysoprasus;** the eleventh, a **jacinth;** the twelfth, an **amethyst.** And the **twelve gates were twelve pearls;** every several gate was of one pearl: and **the street of the city was pure gold, as it were transparent glass.** And I saw no temple therein: for the Lord God Almighty and the Lamb are the temple of it. And the city had no need of the sun, neither of the moon, to shine in it: for **the glory of God did lighten it, and the Lamb is the light thereof.** And the nations of them which are saved shall walk in the light of it: **and the kings of the earth do bring their glory and honour into it.** And the gates of it shall not be shut at all by day: for there shall be no night there. **And they shall bring the glory and honour of the *nations* into it.** And there shall in no wise enter into it any thing that defileth, neither whatsoever worketh abomination, or maketh a lie: But they which are written in the Lamb's book of life [emphasis mine].

As we look at these descriptive Verses, I see no appearance of a group of resurrected flesh and bone bodies. At other places in this Revelation of Jesus Christ, when John made reference to the Lord's people (literally), He never used such terms as we find in these Verses.

Now, we will expand further and see what we can uncover.

In Verses 9–10, we hear John being invited to "Come hither, and I will show thee **the bride, the Lamb's wife.**" John is then taken to a high mountain and shown **"that great city, the Holy Jerusalem descending out of heaven from God."** As we have already mentioned, there has been much controversy through the years on the future home of the bride of Jesus Christ. It would seem to me that the controversy is settled in these two

Verses. If God promised to show John the Lamb's wife, and all that he was shown was the holy Jerusalem (a fifteen-hundred mile cubed city made of pure gold), I think this city would *eternally* house the Lord's church with no difficulty! Surely no one believes God's eternal Saints are made from pure gold (Verse 18). As we take a closer look at this city in Verses 11-16, we are given the dimensions and splendor of this holy New Jerusalem. This New Jerusalem had a wall great and high around it, with twelve gates (three each on the north, south, east, and west) in the wall. At each gate was stationed one angel, and each gate had the name of one of the twelve tribes of the children of Israel. Doesn't sound much like the New Testament church, does it? However, it is interesting to note: the twelve foundations this wall was built upon also had the names of the **twelve apostles** of the Lamb in them.

NOTE: I feel that we should take notice that even in the New Heaven and the New Earth **GOD** differentiates between the Church and Israel (twelve tribes / twelve apostles).

If we look in Ephesians 2:19-22, we will see the **"Spiritual promise"** (during the Grace Dispensation) of what is happening *literally* here in Revelation Chapter 21 where **"all things"** have been made new! We read:

> Now therefore ye are no more strangers and foreigners, but fellow citizens with the saints, and of the household of God; And are built upon the foundation of the apostles and prophets, Jesus Christ himself being the chief cornerstone; In whom all the building fitly framed together groweth unto an holy temple in the Lord: In whom ye also are builded together for an habitation of God through the Spirit.

What God promises in Ephesians Chapter 2 spiritually, He has now *literally* brought to pass in Revelation Chapters 21-22.

We know this period will never end, because **what** the first Adam lost in the first Eden, the last Adam has now recovered (and much more) in **The Last Eden. Praise the Name of Jesus!**

As we continue to look at Revelation Chapter 21, God is telling His beloved people that this city is twelve thousand furlongs cubed.

Let's do the math on this city and see if we can calculate the dimensions in miles. One furlong = 660'.[33] 660'× 12,000 furlongs = 7,920,000' ÷ 5,280' (one mile) = 1500 miles, cubed (length, height, breadth equal).

Now folks, to a country boy born in a small two-room house with no facilities in the hills of Middle Tennessee, **that's a big house!**

NOTE: Someone might be asking themselves right about now: How can God's people do all this *moving,* first from this present Earth to the third Heaven, then back to the Millennial Earth for the Kingdom Dispensation, then to the New Heaven and New Earth?

If it takes natural blood to make us function in this natural body, in that day it will take the Holy Ghost to make all these wonderful things happen in this new Spiritual body which Jesus will give us at the Rapture. After the Rapture, I have no idea how much power the Holy Ghost will produce inside a resurrected Saint. Do you know how much He will produce?

Let's read 1 John 3:2 concerning this Rapture of the Church: "Beloved, *now* are we the sons of God, and it doth not yet appear what we **shall be**: but we know that, when he shall appear, *we shall be like him;* for we shall see him as he is" (emphasis mine).

Well, if resurrected saints are going to be **like Him**, how

---

33. Webster, *American Dictionary of the English Language*

is He? I would think all should concur that Jesus Christ is the same yesterday, today, and forever! (Read Hebrews 13:8). With that said, let's consider this:

» Knowing **He** walked out on death, can we not walk out on death?
» Knowing **He** flew from this present Earth to the third Heaven, can we not fly to the third Heaven?
» Knowing **He** will return in power and great glory, can we not return *with Him* in power and great glory?
» Knowing **He** will reign until He has put all enemies under His feet, can we not reign with Him until He has put all these enemies under His feet?
» Knowing **He** will come *into* this New Heaven, New Earth, and holy New Jerusalem, can we not expect to ***move in*** with Him? Well, can we not?

Hey, folks! Our God is the only God who is alive and well and knows how to get things done. Let me now say: He has all power in Heaven and Earth and certainly does all things, well!

Give Him praise as you continue!

I am persuaded the Rapture, or calling out of the Church, happens in 1 Thessalonians 4:13-18. If my convictions are true and this Rapture does occur pre-Tribulation, then (as already mentioned), all those taken up will have this wonderful body throughout the seventieth week of Daniel, the Millennial Kingdom of Jesus Christ as He sits on David's throne for one thousand years, and now in this New Heaven, New Earth, and holy New Jerusalem where the **meek** have inherited all of these **new things!** (Read Psalm 37:11; Isaiah 11:4; Matthew 5:5.) **God is so good! AMEN.**

However, we must note, again: God is only doing (here in this New Heaven, New Earth, and holy New Jerusalem) what He has desired to do for seven thousand years prior to this time. **He has *at last* brought *His* pure gold tabernacle down in order that He may live with His holy people on this New Earth** (remember Chapter Five), the main difference being that Jesus Christ built this tabernacle, not Moses, not Solomon, not Zerubbabel, not Herod, not Antichrist, not any man or people on this Earth. Just as our Lord Jesus Christ promised in John 14:1-3 to prepare us a place, He has now fulfilled His promise to the most intricate detail!

We read John 14:1-3:

> Let not your hearts be troubled: Ye believe in God, believe also in me. In my Father's house are many mansions: If it were not so, I would have told you. **I go to prepare a place for you. And if I go and prepare a place for you, I will come again, and receive you unto myself; that where I am, there ye may be also** [emphasis mine].

Well, according to Revelation 21:3, Jesus (God in human flesh) is with His people on this New Earth, and we have now *moved* full circle from the First Eden to **The Last Eden.**

Do you know what I think will be the most wonderful thing about this new paradise? We (God's people) will **never** look down the road and see the devil sneaking in to spoil one single thing, as he did in the first paradise, because he has been permanently cast into the lake of fire (read Revelation 20:10). I feel that our father, Adam, and our mother, Eve, will enjoy **The Last Eden** in a way they never were able to enjoy the First Eden. Glory!

I am reluctant to close this manuscript without mentioning **two remaining issues** in these two unique Chapters of God's Holy Scriptures. In my forty-plus years of Bible study, I have yet to hear or read anything satisfactorily covering the text on these **two issues.** Let's read Revelation 21:24,26; 22:2.

And the **nations** of them which are saved shall walk in the light of it [it being New Jerusalem]: And the **kings of the earth** do bring their glory and honour into it. . . . And they shall bring the glory and honour of the **nations** into it. . . . In the midst of the street of it, and on either side of the river, was there the **tree of life**, which bare twelve manner of fruits, and yielded her fruit every month: and the *leaves of the tree* were for the *healing of the nations* [emphasis mine].

Keeping these Verses in mind, let's look at the promises of God to His resurrected, immortal Saints "who have inherited all things" in this new Eden paradise.

In Revelation 21:4-5, John writes of no tears, no death, no sorrow, no crying, no pain, for all former things are passed away and all present things have been made new! Knowing the Words of God are true, I would think these resurrected, immortal Saints being spoken of in Verses 4-5 would not and could not get sick. What do you think? Could they?

Since Revelation 21:24,26; 22:2 informs us there are nations who will receive healing from this tree of life (22:2b—and the leaves of the tree were **for** the healing of the nations), I think an appropriate question would be: First, who are these nations and, second, why will they need this healing? One thing we are definitely assured of: they are saved by God's amazing grace because Revelation 21:24a tells us so!

After looking at all definitions in Hebrew, Greek, and English of this word "nations," I have come to the conclusion that in this land where all things have been made new, definitions are probably new also! Thus, as simply stated: These are the nations of them which are saved (Revelation 21:24a). But this in no way explains their need for healing!

If we went back seven thousand years and read Genesis 2:9, we would find God had a tree of life in His first Eden that he planted for the first Adam. Also, if we read Genesis 3:22-23, we would learn how God had to remove the first Adam (after the fall noted in Chapter One of this manuscript) lest he eat of this tree of life, and **live forever, in his sins.**

However, we must note: This first Adam had blood flowing in his veins, a fact Scriptures prove will not be the case with **resurrected immortal Saints in The Last Eden!** When Jesus left this Earth to return to His Heavenly Father, He had a flesh and bone body, not flesh and blood (Read Luke 24:36-43). **Remember, He gave His blood at Calvary for the sins of the whole world!** We have already noted in this Chapter that Scripture teaches that after the Rapture we will be with Him and like Him. So, what is the answer to the $64,000 question? Who are the nations in question in Revelation 22:2?

I suppose we will leave you, the reader, to decide; but as you are thinking on this mystery, think on this: Is it just possible that God will bring those nations from the Millennium over into **The Last Eden** without making them flesh and bone immortals as raptured Saints will be? Is it just possible that He will leave them, sinless, mortal, flesh and blood as our Father Adam was in the First Eden, prior to his fall into sin? Also, as you are thinking on this mystery, remember the Matthew Chapter 25 judgment. All living nations who went to the right hand of Jesus Christ came into this Millennial Kingdom **in natural bodies.** If Adam could have eaten of the tree of life in the First Eden and lived in a natural body forever (in his sins), what is to hinder our God from bringing the Millennial Saints who are in natural bodies into **The Last Eden** to, forever enjoy healing leaves from this tree of life in their natural bodies? Is anyone to say that our Holy God cannot do with His own as He pleases?

One thing is for sure. Our Holy God did have a good sense of humor to write the Holy Scriptures as He did, in order to make you and I dig to find many of the answers. But there is one thing He wrote that no man need be confused about: Jesus Christ *freely* paid our sin debt in full.

Note: Before I close this final Chapter, I would like to share a quote from Brother Ken Ham's great book, *The Lie: Evolution*. In this treasure of information on the ills of evolution, we pull out these two awesome paragraphs:

> If we want to come to right conclusions about anything, the only sure way would be to **start with the Word of the One who has absolute knowledge.**
>
> We Christians must build all our thinking in every area *on the Bible*. We must judge what people say on the basis of what God's Word says: not the other way around [emphasis mine].

I am thoroughly convinced that, instead of reading the commentaries at the bottom of the pages of our Bibles and taking them for inspired truth, Christians need to get back to the pure Words of our Holy God and begin *anew* to investigate what God did over the last six thousand years to prove His undying love for the Adam race! I have humbly attempted to do just a small portion of that investigation in this short manuscript. I pray that my investigation has spurred your thinking and you will do a more thorough investigation on your own from God's inspired text.

For our final Scriptures, we will read 1 John 5:7-13. (Note: Verse 7 is excluded from many perverted Bible versions).

> For there are three that bear record in Heaven, the Father, the Word, and the Holy Ghost: and **these three are one**. And there are three that bear witness in earth, the Spirit, and the

water, and the blood: and these three **agree in one.** If we receive the witness of men, the witness of God is greater: for this is the witness of God which he hath testified of his Son. He that believeth on the Son of God **hath the witness in himself:** He that believeth not God hath made him a liar; because he believeth not the record that God gave of his Son. And this is the record, **that God has given unto us eternal life, and this life is in his Son. He that hath the Son hath life; and he that hath not the Son hath not life. These things have I written unto you that believe on the name of the Son of God; that ye may *know* that ye have eternal life, and that ye may believe on the name of the Son of God** [emphasis mine].

It is my sincere prayer you have enjoyed your journey in this manuscript from the First Eden to **The Last Eden**, and that you have made your Spiritual reservations for this future paradise. If you have not made your Spiritual reservations, you can do so when God calls you by His Holy Spirit. When this call comes, *a slow response* could cause you to miss *going* **Beyond the Revelation into The Last Eden!**

—Elder, Terry Gayle Alexander

Epilogue

Revelation
The Book of Sevens

As we bring our work to a close, I thought I would offer for your consideration this last thought on this final Book of the Bible. Without this precious Book of Revelation, many of the Old and New Testament prophecies would go unanswered in the minds and hearts of God's people. With this Book, our excitement and expectations grow each day as we await our next big event in prophecy: the Rapture of the Church to meet the Lord Jesus Christ in the air!

This Book of Revelation truly is God's crowning jewel of Prophecy, and I thank God for giving it to John in order that he might write what he saw in a book, sending it unto the seven churches which were in Asia. God then honored your life and mine by preserving this Book of Revelation as the last Book in the canon of Scripture.

With "eight" being the Biblical number of **new beginnings**, and "Eight" being the number of Chapters in this manuscript, please, consider these eight "sevens" taking us through this wonderful Book to go **Beyond the Revelation** into the gracious New Heaven and New Earth our God has created for Himself and all of His redeemed children. AMEN!

1. Seven Churches (Revelation 2-3).
SEVEN STARS are the SEVEN ANGELS of the SEVEN CHURCH-

ES. SEVEN CANDLESTICKS are THE SEVEN CHURCHES (Revelation 1:20). There are those who sum up these seven churches in this manner:

» 1st church—Ephesus: apostolic age ends (Revelation 2:1-7)
» 2nd church—Smyrna: great persecutions (Revelation 2:8-11)
» 3rd church—Pergamos: settled in the world (Revelation 2:12-17)
» 4th church—Thyatira: believing remnant (Revelation 2:18-29)
» 5th church—Sardis: reformation remnant (Revelation 3:1-6)
» 6th church—Philadelphia: true church in the professing church (Revelation 3:7-13)
» 7th church—Laodicea: apostasy; the worldly churches' final state (Revelation 3:14-22)

2. Seven Seals (Revelation 6:1-17; 8:1)

» 1st Seal—White horse rider: conquering (Revelation 6:1-2)
» 2nd Seal—Red horse rider: peace taken from the Earth (Revelation 6:3-4)
» 3rd Seal—Black horse rider: famine in the Earth (Revelation 6:5-6)
» 4th Seal—Pale horse rider: quarter of Earth's population killed (Revelation 6:7-8)
» 5th Seal—Martyrs in Heaven encouraged and given white robes (Revelation 6:9-11)
» 6th Seal—Great wrath intensifies on Earth; mountains move; men hide (Revelation 6:12-17)

» 7th Seal—Silence in Heaven about half hour; seven trumpets begin (Revelation 8:1-6)

3. Seven Trumpets (Revelation 8:2-13; 9:1-21; 11:15-19)

» 1st Trumpet—one-third of all trees, all green grass burnt up (Revelation 8:7)
» 2nd Trumpet—one-third of the sea became blood; one-third of creatures in the sea dies; one-third of the ships were destroyed (Revelation 8:8-9)
» 3rd Trumpet—one-third of the fresh waters become wormwood (Revelation 8:10-11)
» 4th Trumpet—one-third of the sun, moon, and stars smitten (Revelation 8:12-13)
» 5th Trumpet—Angel opens the bottomless pit; mankind tormented five months (Revelation 9:1-12)
» 6th Trumpet—four angels loosed in the river Euphrates; one-third of mankind dies (Revelation 9:13-21)

4. Seven Thunders—Uttered between Trumpet Six and Seven (Revelation 10:3-4)

Note: No one *outside the Holy God in Heaven* understands what these seven thunders hold. Nevertheless, they are an integral part of this Book of Revelation, because they are in the text. Someone could ask, "When will we know what the seven thunders uttered?" I would lovingly say, "For now we see through a glass, darkly: but then face to face: Now I know in part, but, then, shall I know even as, also, I am known (1 Corinthians 13:12). **Praise his Name!**

» 1st Thunder—SEALED
» 2nd Thunder—SEALED
» 3rd Thunder—SEALED

» 4th Thunder—SEALED
» 5th Thunder—SEALED
» 6th Thunder—SEALED
» 7th Thunder—SEALED

» 7th Trumpet: Judgments Resumed—announcement made by the seventh angel: "**The kingdoms of this world are become the kingdoms of our Lord and of his Christ**; and he shall reign forever and forever" (Revelation 11:15). (Note Revelation 10:7.)

5. Seven Personages (Revelation 12:1-17; 13:1-18)
» 1st Personage—The woman, Israel (Revelation 12:1-2)
» 2nd Personage—Satan (Revelation 12:3-4; 12:6,13-17)
» 3rd Personage—The Man-Child, Jesus Christ (Revelation 12:5)
» 4th Personage—The archangel, Michael (Revelation 12:7)
» 5th Personage—The Jewish remnant (Revelation 12:17)
» 6th Personage—The Beast out of the sea (Revelation 13:1-10)
» 7th Personage—The Beast out of the Earth (Revelation 13:11-18)

6. Seven Vials (Revelation 15:7)
» 1st Vial—Sore on beast worshipers (Revelation 16:2)
» 2nd Vial—Sea became blood; all sea life dies (Revelation 16:3)
» 3rd Vial—All rivers and waters become blood (Revelation 16:4-7)
» 4th Vial—Men scorched with the heat of the sun; no repentance (Revelation 16:8-9)
» 5th Vial—Kingdom of the beast full of darkness; no repen-

tance (Revelation 16:10-11)
- » 6th Vial—Euphrates dried up; way for Eastern kings prepared (Revelation 16:12)
- » 7th Vial—It is done: voices, thunders, lightning, and an earthquake such as was not since men were upon the Earth. Every island and mountain leveled; falling hail, every stone about the weight of a talent (approximately 50 to 100 pounds[34] in weight; God is blasphemed (Revelation 16:17-21). Note: Attic talent = 56 pounds, 11ounces. Hebrew talent of silver = 113 pounds, 10 ounces.[35]

7. Seven Dooms (Revelation 17-20)
- » 1st Doom—The doom of Babylon (Revelation 17:1-18:24)
- » 2nd Doom—The doom of the Beast (Revelation 19:19-20)
- » 3rd Doom—The doom of the False Prophet (Revelation 19:20)
- » 4th Doom—The doom of the kings and their armies (Revelation 19:17-19; 21)
- » 5th Doom—The doom of Gog and Magog **after the thousand years** (Revelation 20:7-9)
- » 6th Doom—The doom of Satan **after the thousand years** (Revelation 20:10)
- » 7th Doom—The doom of the unbelieving dead **after the thousand years** (Revelation 20:11-15)

8. Seven New Things After the Thousand Years (Revelation 21:1; 22:7)
1. The New Heaven (Revelation 21:1)
2. The New Earth (Revelation 21:1)
3. The New Peoples (Revelation 21:3-8)
4. The New Jerusalem (REvelation 21:9-21

---
34. Butler, *Holman Bible Dictionary*
35. Webster, *American Dictionary of the English Language*

5. The New Temple—Revelation 21:22
6. The New Light—Revelation 21:23-27
7. **The New Paradise—Revelation 22:1-7—THE LAST EDEN!**

"Seven" is the number used more than any number in the Bible besides the number "one." In the Biblical numeric, our LORD took the **perfect world number, "four,"** and added **the divine number, "three,"** to come up with the number of **divine completeness: "seven."** When we read of the **seventh** seven (seven dooms), we realize **all things concerning this present Earth** are completely finished. But as our God is full of marvelous grace, that is not the end of the story.

As already stated, eight is the number of new beginnings,[36] thus the eighth "seven" (seven new things).

This brings us into God's final glory world (the new paradise, **The Last Eden), the prepared place that Jesus Christ promised in John Chapter 14. Just as God started Adam and Eve in paradise (Eden), so He will bring all His Saints back to paradise, to this New Heaven and New Earth. Then and only then will Heaven be Heaven to all who have believed to the saving of the soul (Hebrews 10:39). Glory to the Son of GOD!**

—Elder Terry Gayle Alexander

---

36. Hutchings, *Master Mathematician*

Addendum A

Temples in Scripture

It is quite interesting to note in Scripture all of the emphasis the Lord has placed on temples. We are reminded of this in Chapter Five of this manuscript as we see Joseph gathering and Moses removing the wealth of Egypt in order for God to build the tabernacle in the wilderness. It would seem from the evidence in Scripture this program of gathering wealth to build temples is definitely a priority with God as we have shown.

The Bible records **ten great Scriptural temples: five physical structural temples, and five fleshly or spiritual temples. We will now attempt to examine these ten great Scriptural temples from the Words of God.**

1. **The Tabernacle in the wilderness**—set up by Moses around 1445 B.C.[37] We read in Exodus 40:17,34,38: "And it came to pass in the first month in the second year, on the first day of the month, that the tabernacle was reared up. . . . Then a cloud covered the tent of the congregation, and the **glory of the LORD filled the tabernacle**. . . . For the **cloud** of the LORD was upon the tabernacle by day, and **fire** was on it by night, in the sight of all the house of Israel,

---

37. Ussher, James. *The Annals of the World*

throughout **all** their journeys.

2. **The First Temple**—erected by Solomon in approximately 959 B.C.[38] We read of this event in 1 Kings 7:51; 8:4. "So was ended all the work that king Solomon made for the house of the LORD. And Solomon brought in the things which David his father had dedicated; even the silver, and the gold, and the vessels, did he put among the treasures of the house of the LORD..... And they brought up the ark of the LORD, and the tabernacle of the congregation, and all the Holy vessels that were in the tabernacle, even those did the priests and the Levites bring up."

3. **The Second Temple**—built by Zerubbabel around 516 B.C.[39] and, enlarged and beautified by Herod around 10 B.C.[40] In Ezra 6:14–15 and John 2:20, we read: "And the elders of the Jews builded, and they prospered through the prophesying of Haggai the prophet and Zechariah the son of Iddo. And they builded, and finished it, according to the commandment of the God of Israel, and according to the commandment of Cyrus, and Dairus, and Artaxerxes king of Persia. And this house was finished on the third day of the month Adar, which was in the sixth year of the reign of Dairus the king." "Then said the Jews, Forty and six years was this temple in building, and wilt thou rear it up in three days?"

4. **The Third Temple** is to be built sometime in the future (possibly by the Antichrist) before the middle of Daniel's seventieth week. We read in Matthew 24:15: "When ye therefore shall see the abomination of desolation, spoken of by Daniel the prophet, stand in the holy place, (whoso readeth, let him understand)." We then look into Daniel

---
38. Ibid.
39. Ibid.
40. Ibid.

to see the Words of God Daniel spoke. In Daniel 9:27 we read: "And he [the Antichrist] shall confirm the covenant with many for **one week:** and in the **midst of the week** he shall cause the **sacrifice and oblation to cease,** and for the overspreading of abominations he shall make it desolate. In the Book of Daniel, this "one week" is in reality "seven years." So, the Antichrist will stop the sacrifice and oblation, and desolate the Holy Place in the middle of the seven years, leaving forty-two months until the end of the seven-year period. John then picks up this subject in Revelation 11:1-2. We read: "And there was given me a reed, like unto a rod: and the angel stood, saying, rise and **measure the temple of God,** and the altar, and them that worship therein. But the court which is without the temple leave out, and measure it not; for it is given unto the Gentiles: and the holy city shall they tread under foot forty and two months. It is easy to see a temple must be built prior to the last half of this seven-year period, which is forty-two months, in order that this Antichrist might reign until he is destroyed by the true Christ at His return recorded in Revelation 19:11-21.

5. **The Millennial Temple** to be built by our Lord and Savior Christ Jesus at the beginning of the Millennium. If we study the prophetic implications of Zechariah 6:12-13, we will surely come to the conclusion that this man **"whose name is the BRANCH"** is *not* making reference to the Joshua mentioned in Verse 11. We read: "And speak unto him, saying, Thus speaketh the LORD of hosts, saying, Behold the man whose name is the BRANCH; and he shall grow up out of His place, and **he shall build the temple of the LORD:** Even he shall build the temple of the LORD; and he shall bear the glory, and **shall sit and rule upon his throne;** and he shall be a priest upon his throne: and

the counsel of peace shall be between them both (Zechariah 6:12-13). We should notice that this personal name BRANCH is totally capitalized in these Holy Scriptures, just as the word LORD is totally capitalized. **I would now like to examine the Scriptures and note the examples of how God uses this name BRANCH in future prophetic settings to denote His Son, Christ Jesus.** In Isaiah 4:2-3a we read: "In that day shall the BRANCH of the LORD be beautiful and glorious, and the fruit of the earth shall be excellent and comely for them that are escaped of Israel. And it shall come to pass, that he that is left in Zion, and he that remaineth in Jerusalem, shall be called holy." In Jeremiah 33:14-17 we find these Words: "Behold, the days come, saith the LORD, that I will perform **that good thing** which I have promised unto the house of Israel and to the house of Judah. In those days, and at that time, will I cause the **BRANCH of righteousness** to grow up unto David; and he shall execute judgment and righteousness in the land. In those days shall **Judah be saved, and Jerusalem shall dwell safely;** and this is the name wherewith she [Jerusalem] shall be called, The LORD our righteousness. For thus saith the LORD, David shall never want a man to sit upon the throne of the house of Israel." Jeremiah 23:3-8 gives us more insight into this Branch of David. We read: "And I will gather the remnant of my flock out of all countries whither I have driven them, and will bring them again to their folds; and they shall be fruitful and increase. And I will set up shepherds over them which shall feed them: and they shall fear no more, nor be dismayed, neither shall they be lacking saith the LORD. Behold the days come, saith the LORD, that I will raise unto David a righteous **BRANCH**, and a king shall reign and prosper, and shall execute judgment and justice **in the earth**. In His days [the King's days]

Judah shall be saved, and Israel shall dwell safely: and this is the name [the King's name] whereby he shall be called, THE LORD OUR RIGHTEOUSNESS. Therefore, behold, the days come, saith the LORD, that they shall no more say, The LORD liveth, which brought up the children of Israel out of the land of Egypt; But, The LORD liveth, which brought up and which led the seed of the house of Israel **out of the north country, and from all countries whither I had driven them; and they** [the house of Israel] **shall dwell in their own land.**" In Zechariah 3:8, **we read:** "Hear now, O Joshua the high priest, thou, and thy fellows that sit before thee: for they are men wondered at: for, behold, I will bring forth My servant the **BRANCH**." I feel we have sufficient evidence in these many prophetic Scriptures to show that this **BRANCH** mentioned in Zechariah 6:12 is, in reality, **Christ Jesus the Lord,** and that He shall build the temple of the LORD at the beginning of the Millennium. AMEN!

6. **The Body of Jesus,** which was prepared by the Father and brought into the world at Bethlehem through the virgin Mary. We read in Hebrews 10:5 of this most important event: "Wherefore when he cometh into the world, he saith, Sacrifice and offering thou wouldest not, but a body hast thou prepared me." Then in John 2:21 we find that this body of Jesus is referred to as a temple. We read: "But He spake of **the temple of His body.**"

7. **The Bride of Christ** prepared by the Holy Spirit. In 1 Corinthians 12:12–14 we read: "For as the body is one, and hath many members, and all the members of that one body, being many, are one body: so also is Christ. For **by one Spirit** are we all baptized into one body whether we be Jews or Gentiles, whether we be bond or free: and have been all made to drink **into one Spirit.** For the body is not one member, but many." We then learn in Ephesians

2:19-22 that this bride of Christ is in reality a temple for the habitation of God through the Spirit. We read: "Now therefore ye are no more strangers and foreigners, but fellowcitizens with the saints, and of the household of God, and are built upon the foundation of the apostles and the prophets, Jesus Christ himself being the chief cornerstone. In whom all the building fitly framed together groweth unto **an holy temple in the Lord:** In whom ye also are builded together **for an habitation of God through the Spirit."**

8. **The body of the believer** prepared by the Holy Spirit at the moment of conversion. We read in 1Corinthians 3:16-17: "Know ye not that **ye are the temple of God,** and that the Spirit of God dwelleth in you? If any man defile the temple of God, him shall God destroy: for the temple of God is holy, **which temple ye are."**

9. **The temple of God** in the present third Heaven where God now dwells. We find this temple mentioned in Revelation 11:19. We read: "And the **temple of God** was opened **in heaven,** and there was seen **in his temple the ark of his** *testament:* and there were lightnings, and thunderings, and an earthquake, and great hail." This Verse could also answer the age-old question of what happened to the **ark of the** *covenant.* God simply took it to His temple in the present third Heaven, where the Apostle John was permitted to view it from the Isle of Patmos when he saw the heavenly vision and recorded God's Words. Note: *Diatheke* is the word in Greek[41] for both "covenant" and "testament."

10. **The Temple of God** in the New Heaven and the New Earth. We read in Revelation 21:3: "And I heard a great voice out of heaven saying, Behold the tabernacle [dwelling place]

---

41. Strong, *Exhaustive Concordance*

of God is with men, and he will dwell with them, and they shall be his people, and God himself shall be with them, and be their God." Then we read in Revelation 21:22 these Words: "And I saw no temple therein [speaking of New Jerusalem] **for the Lord God Almighty and the Lamb are the temple of it."** It would seem when this present Earth, Heaven, and Jerusalem are destroyed by dissolving fire, and the New Heaven, Earth, and holy Jerusalem come into view, our God and His Son will be the only temple necessary for all eternity. We also learn there will be no need for the sun or moon to shine, because the Father and Jesus will light everything with their glory. In that glorious world (New Heaven and New Earth), it seems we will finally tabernacle "in **The Last Eden,**" that being every one that is written in the Lamb's Book of Life. Glory to our revealing God!!!

—Elder Terry Gayle Alexander

Addendum B

Born Again?

As we look and listen in these last days, it could be very confusing as to what we hear and see concerning the teachings about being born again. In John 3:3, we read these Words of our Saviour Jesus Christ: "Jesus answered and said unto him [Nicodemus], Verily, verily, I say unto thee, except a man be born again, he cannot see the kingdom of God."

Jesus then continues in John 3:5-7 with these Words: "Verily, verily, I say unto thee, except a man be born of water and of the Spirit, he cannot enter into the kingdom of God. That which is born of the flesh is flesh; and that which is born of the Spirit is Spirit. Marvel not that I said unto thee, Ye must be born again."

If we look in the old 1828 *Noah Webster's Dictionary,* we find this definition for the word "again." It simply means, "a second time; once more."

As we take a closer look at John 3:6 we see a very revealing statement by our Saviour. "That which is born of the flesh, is flesh; that which is born of the Spirit, is Spirit."

Not many years back (as a loved one of mine was being lowered into the grave at a local cemetery), I heard a shipped in, apostate preacher say with true satisfaction, "Sister ????? is now truly born again." This ignorant apostate did not know that this sister was *truly* born again on an old-time altar bench at a local Baptist church long before he was born into this world.

Many songs (as well as many preachers and teachers) often give the suggestion that we must first get into Heaven before we are born again. This greatly enhances their agenda on legalism and salvation by works. Such people teach that you must make the balance (to the right) at the judgment scales of God before you can truly know the end result of God's promises. The religion of Islam also teaches the same, but there could be nothing farther from the truth. In fact, just the opposite is taught in the true Words of God. First Peter 1:22-23 gives us this insight on the matter. We read: "Seeing ye have purified your souls in obeying the truth through the Spirit unto unfeigned love of the brethren, see that ye love one another with a pure heart fervently: Being born again, not of corruptible seed, but of incorruptible, by the Word of God, which liveth and abideth forever."

I wonder what it means to be born of incorruptible seed. Well, just one look in our old *Webster's Dictionary* leaves us no doubt. We read: "Incorruptible: That cannot corrupt or decay: Not admitting of corruption."

First John 4:6-7 continues with this same thought. We read: "We are of God; he that knoweth God heareth us; he that is not of God heareth not us. Hereby know we the spirit of truth and the spirit of error. Beloved, let us love one another: for love is of God; and every one that loveth is **born of God, and knoweth God.**"

Do Saints have to wait until they get to Heaven to love one another? I don't think so. John 17:3 states: "And this is life eternal, that they may know thee: the only true God and Jesus Christ, whom thou hast sent." John 10:14 continues with these words: "I am the good shepherd, and know my sheep, and am known of mine."

So the question is, my friend: Do you know God personally?

What would cause men and women today to think that they must first get to Heaven before they can be born again when Jesus made it very clear to Nicodemus that you must be born again before you can see the Kingdom? It is the same miserable monster that existed when Christ was on earth—unbelief. As a Christian, when we get to the judgment Christ will be meting out judgment to determine rewards, not to determine eternal life. See 1 Corinthians 3:9-15; 2 Corinthians 5:10.

First John 3:9, 5:18 makes the new birth so plain that no one should miss the simplicity of the inner and outer man. Listen as the pure Word of God divides the natural and the spiritual. We read: "Whosoever is born of God doth not commit sin; for his seed [God's Seed] remaineth in him; and he cannot sin, because he is born of God (3:9). "We know that whosoever is born of God sinneth not; but he that is begotten of God [Jesus Christ] keepeth himself, and that wicked one toucheth him not" (5:18).

In these two Verses, Who is this Man *in the believer* that is begotten of God and is keeping Himself? Who is this Man *in the believer* that does not commit sin? Who is this Man *in the believer* that is the Seed of God and is also remaining *in everyone* that is born again? Who is this Man *in the believer* that the wicked one cannot even touch? Who is this Man *in the believer* that is Spirit (John 3:6)? No one should miss this mystery: "To whom God would make known what is the riches of the glory of this mystery among the Gentiles; which is, Christ in you the hope of glory" (Colossians 1:27) **PRAISE GOD!**

That which is born of the Spirit is Spirit. The Man *in the believer* is Christ, and for your soul's sake *both now and in the future* please make sure He is in you NOW! [all scriptural emphasis and commentary mine.]

In Closing

As I look back over this journey "from the First Eden to **The Last Eden**," I realize we have only touched a small portion of the subject matter contained in history and the Scriptures. I think the Gospel of John says it best in John 21:25: "And there are also many other things which Jesus did, the which, if they should be written every one, I suppose that even the world itself could not contain the books that should be written. Amen."

To be able to attempt to write about the great and awesome power of God and His ability to bring these things to pass in order to preserve Adam and his offspring is almost more than I can grasp!

Knowing that sin is the most offensive thing our God has to deal with in His universe, it causes me to stand in awe when I think of God going to such lengths to preserve a good seed from Adam to Mary. Also, He has promised to preserve His Saints from the moment of conversion to the end of the world. (See Matthew 28:20.)

Had this only begotten Son of God **not** been born perfect from His mother's womb, then all of the human family would have been lost to Satan and his wicked devices! However, as I said in the manuscript, God moved, Joseph waited, Mary believed, Jesus was born! And may I say, He was born perfect! **He *is* the only begotten Son of God!**

There are many views concerning the fallen angels in Genesis Chapter 6. However, the view we have presented (fallen embodied angels cohabiting with Adamic women) is the only view giving a sensible reason for the gene pool to have been altered, producing a world of mighty giants who were perverse. As I look at this world in motion, there just may be another outbreak in the making!

I realize I have missed some of the many attempts of Lucifer to stop this perfect seed (from Adam to Mary); however, I hope you will make your own private study on those not listed in this manuscript. I also pray you have been enlightened *anew* at just how much God loves you and orchestrated these many events for your personal benefit and preservation!

If you have not made your peace-calling and election sure, do so the moment God calls you! You cannot go to be with Jesus and enter this Last Eden on a technicality! Ye must be born again. (Read 2 Peter 1:10-11; John 3:3-7.)

—In Christian Love,
Elder Terry Gayle Alexander